I am Me,
No One Special

I Am Me, No One Special

Copyright © Valerie Mulcare-Tivey 2018 All Rights Reserved

The rights of Valerie Mulcare-Tivey to be identified as the author of this work have been asserted in accordance with the Copyright, Designs and Patents Act 1988

Spiderwize
Remus House
Coltsfoot Drive
Woodston
Peterborough
PE2 9BF

www.spiderwize.com

A CIP catalogue record for this book is available from the British Library.

The views expressed in this work are solely those of the author and do not necessarily reflect the views of the publisher, and the publisher hereby disclaims any responsibility for them.

ISBN: 978-1-912694-67-9

eBook ISBN: 978-1-912694-68-6

I AM ME, NO ONE SPECIAL

Valerie Mulcare-Tivey

SPIDERWIZE
Peterborough UK
2018

I Am Me, No One Special

Is dedicated to

Family and every branch of our
extended family new and old.

Dear friends all over the world.

Children, who should only ever be safe and loved.

Cherry dog for putting up with my singing.

Special dedications to Daniel Robinson,
my cousin Cheryl, Jordan, and Steve.

Everyone else whom we cherish that
passed tragically to spirit.

Contents

CHAPTER ONE

'P' for Positive

As the Queen of Procrastination, the 'P' word is one I dislike intensely. Yet true to form umming and aaaaahing about whether or not to write this particular type of book I faffed around like an adrenaline fuelled ferret but why? Writing fills my soul with passion and all things spiritual are as much a part of me as my heartbeat, therefore it will be easy to share spiritual experiences with you. So changing the 'P' word to Positive my aim is to comfort and reassure those of you curious but new to the intriguing world of spirit and angels. This book has been a long time coming, yet in the grand scheme of things especially related to spirit there is order, that in mind the timing is spot on and it feels right. With rapidly growing interest in the afterlife and angelic realm, scepticism is being replaced by intrigue, trust and belief. It is no longer a taboo subject; spirituality is being wholeheartedly embraced, previously scornful doubters becoming faithful believers. From a very early age I have for whatever reason been able to connect with spirit bringing forth amazing experiences but not knowing anything different I never considered then that this was a very special gift to be blessed with because *I Am Me, No One Special*.

It all seemed normal and I often giggled when my mother spoke of Grandma Willis, the seventh child of a seventh child whose weird and wonderful behaviour was classed as eccentricity but was in fact powerful clairvoyance. Tales of Grandma Willis made me love her dearly even though she had passed long before my early morning entrance to the world had occurred, almost head first into the toilet bowl to be precise. Bless her heart, I have always felt an affinity and even though Grandma was lovingly referred to as a tadge batty she and I would no doubt have been kindred spirits. Sharing a few of my stories will be a huge pleasure and hopefully you will take something good from each one to help you along the sometimes very harsh highway of life. They are randomly picked from a massive library of events stored in my memory. I must warn you though that remembering dates isn't my forte and not forward seeing the need to remember, I rarely scribbled notes. Daft really not to know in advance, something so obvious with such an accessible gift but in the grand scheme of things not vital. There is some semblance of order, and I hope to show you clearly, how family and friends in spirit and loving angels have been a guiding light throughout life, enabling me to help people. Everything always seemed to sit right, regardless of when, where and how.

CHAPTER TWO

Babies Have Memories Too

This first story may seem rather far-fetched, indeed had someone related it to me I would probably have found difficulty in believing it. Simply because when this event happened, I was a baby of around five months old, too young at the time to make more than a few simple sounds in lieu of words. Definitely unable to relate at the time what I had witnessed, yet astonishingly several years later was able to tell the story with total recall, describing events with such accurate detail that my mother could not stop shaking. That was perhaps my earliest recall of anything as significant as this happening to other people.

The pram that I was in felt soothingly bouncy and as we spoke about that day years later my mother told me that the pram was a beautiful Silver Cross classic design with spring suspension. Evidently the Rolls Royce of prams in those days and her face positively glowed with pride as she described it, our mother was always 'Mummy' the loving mummy whose children were her world and just about everything had to be perfect for us.

In those days, bearing in mind that I am now happy Granny Lipstick to a wonderful little brood, mothers didn't have any qualms about leaving their baby parked outside a shop in the pram. Thus, I was duly parked next to a sloping path that zig zagged up to a grey stone building with a wooden hand rail all along the left hand wall. My mother was wearing maroon red high heels and I watched as she disappeared into the building that I later learned was a Post Office. Kicking off my left shoe and sock, a chubby bare foot crept from under the pram covers to paddle in the rain water collected on the outer waterproof cover. Soon after, my mother tucked the stray foot back beneath the covers before playfully telling me off.

I clearly remembered a lady approaching her; they hugged and chatted before she was invited to go home with us. The pram was wheeled into our big welcoming kitchen and I watched with curious interest as my mother made a pot of tea for her guest. Of course, it was all done properly back then with lovely china tea sets and biscuits that were arranged nicely on doilies to dress the plates. Following tea, the next act of kindness was to pack up a huge bag of groceries and home baking plus tokens to exchange for milk and fresh orange juice. Tokens were given to new mothers for post birth nourishment; Mum gave hers to the lady without hesitation or thought for her own health. My mother then went upstairs to find a warm coat for the lady and I watched the lady open Mum's handbag taking out several folded ten shilling notes before furtively stuffing them into her own pockets. The sad thing is that had this 'so called' friend asked for money it would have been given to her with love. Instead when my brother Peter came home we watched Mum sob as though her heart would break when she discovered the cold callous theft from right under her nose. Peter is three years older than me and being unable to help or comfort our kind beautiful mother during her sadness was awful for him, our father was overseas in the Royal Air Force. Years later when I relived the whole scenario in clear detail to my mother she told me that everything I saw that day as a baby happened as described, even down to what she and the lady were wearing.

CHAPTER THREE

Banished Shamefully To My Bedroom

When I was a very small child my mother had discovered the unusual gift bestowed upon me for no apparent reason and was fully accepting of it. That was when she decided to tell me about Grandma Willis, there was obviously good reasoning behind Mummy telling me about her great grandmother and the significance became clearer as the years passed by. Being the seventh daughter of a seventh daughter is very powerful spiritually and Grandma Willis was extremely gifted, this was at a time when such things were taboo and not mentioned, mainly because they were scorned as work of the Devil. I truly believe that I was being given permission by my mother to be myself and it was her way of saying it was okay to be different. Grandma stories were comforting, and as far as spiritual events go were a big influence. In fact, Grandma Jane Eleanor in spirit changed the whole direction of my life and has guided me ever since as you will see later, it was a profound event that made me see without a scrap of doubt what I was meant to do. *I Am Me, No One Special*, but I do have a special gift that makes me forever grateful.

The kitchen was warm and smelled of freshly baked jam tarts, cinnamon apple pies and fruity scones. Mum and I were up to our necks in baking paraphernalia with clouds of flour swirling as she dusted down the smaller baking board in front of me. My contribution to the bake fest was to be gingerbread men, at last I could get my hands on the lovely squidgy pastry mixture. Both parents attempted to equip us with simple cookery skills but as children our culinary offerings were not the most appetising. Still, moments like that were loved and cherished, more happy memories for my mental library. Mum was singing along to the radio, I was happy because life was good, and Peter appeared equally happy as he tucked into the broken bits of biscuit mix. He was making roads for his Dinky cars while nibbling and humming at the same time, we felt loved without any doubt our home was a haven of happiness. Sharon, our sister one year younger than me had woken from her nap in the cat's basket and was gratefully accepting bits of biscuit from Peter, our hero. The secure bliss of that moment was about to change, rolling out the by then grubby piece of pastry I reached for the man shaped cutter, collected currants to form eyes then froze on the spot.

Staring at Mum I calmly stated 'Mummy, Grandma Daisy just died, she came and said hello to me'. 'Valerie!!! go to your room this minute, that was a cruel and horrible thing to say' she said crossly. My mother's beautifully arched eyebrows rose with dramatic effect, her expression had changed from that of shock to anger as she had uttered her command with force. Protesting loudly, I climbed down from the stool and walked from the kitchen, muttering under the cross glare following each laboured step. 'She did die Mummy' I retorted, it fell on deaf ears, I was banished shamefully, and happy baking time was over. Cross mother, rumbling tummy not surprisingly from hunger but the lost expectation of crumbly delicious baking to nibble.

Why? I wondered, was it so wrong to tell Mum what Grandma Daisy had told me to say, I was an honest little girl and was puzzled by how cross our gentle kind mother was. It wasn't quite midday, I had dressed at least twenty of the vast collection of dolls sharing my room and decided to wander downstairs, surely my outburst was forgiven, after all it wasn't that bad was it? My mother's unyielding expression of disappointment spoke volumes, her eyes could perform a whole play without a word being spoken, Mum had perfected 'the look'. Fortunately, we were not the usual recipients of that expression it was a look well-honed and reserved for people who have been unkind to someone. I was handed a plate of cheese and crackers with the knowledge that my only option was to trot back upstairs to my bedroom. Not exactly prison like, with everything pretty and tastefully chosen or made by the beautiful lady with arched eyebrows who at that moment really did not like me. Feeling really miffed it was hard to understand why people thought that I could make things like that up when my own ears hear the voices. It was okay though, because Grandma Daisy explained that Mummy would soon understand, Grandma said that she would come back to see me, she asked me not to be cross with my mother but to give her lots of cuddles. Mid-afternoon, punishment still dragging on I was sitting at the top of our main stairs holding my treasured Rosebud doll when Mum cried out 'please no! don't come here'.

The official knock on the back-porch door was loudly precise, denying the couriers presence would have been futile, our house was gated so anyone entering the grounds came to see us. Looking out of the kitchen window Mum had seen a young man walking up the kitchen garden drive. Wearing a dark sombre uniform there was a small satchel strapped across his chest, he was pushing a moped probably standard issue, she knew that Post Office Telegram messengers often were the bearers of bad news. Mum cried as she was handed the yellow telegram, the young man used to the emotional displays his deliveries often brought about touched her arm awkwardly in a brief show of empathy. No reply required, issuing barely heard words of condolence as he replaced the cap he had taken off in respect the courier let himself out. Hands shaking as she held the telegram, reading the unwanted words over again Mum knelt to cuddle the three of us close to her as she sobbed. Grandma Daisy was her beloved step mum and she adored her, we all did and so we sobbed together. Mum realised that Grandma had died at the exact minute I had informed her that morning. 'Valderee Valderar (her pet name for me) you have a very special gift, I am sorry for doubting you darling and will never doubt you again.' From that day until the day she herself passed my mother supported my spiritual gift 100% and always encouraged me to be creative. Sharon sat tormenting the cat (he loved a challenge), she probably wondered what on earth the fuss was about, how lovely that over the years she has been and still is one of the most loyal and loving people in my life.

CHAPTER FOUR

You Can't Beat A Bit Of Déjà Vu

I remember as a child having love for everyone and because of my father's RAF postings overseas we as a family travelled the world, we had dearly loved friends of practically every race, creed and colour. It was a true blessing to have such a fabulous multitude of culture to learn from and enjoy. For those who have never been given that opportunity or haven't managed to embrace the amazing people who for whatever reason enter our life, it saddens me. Does it seem self-obsessed or 'up myself' as the expression goes to even think of saying this? from childhood I believed that I was sent to earth for a reason, my duty of care, why would I even dare to contemplate that? after all *I Am Me, No One Special*. Inner me has always had the longing need to care for, nurture and cherish people especially those who are vulnerable.

Little was I to know that many years on from the pram outside the post office and Grandma Daisy's passing, I would get to fulfil so many dreams.

One of which was to look after children who have never known a father like ours, who put sooty foot prints in the hearth near to our Christmas sacks. Mince pie crumbs and a half empty sherry glass completed the picture (what a coincidence that it was Harvey's Bristol Cream, one of mum's favourites). All before responding with laughter to our eager shouts of 'has he been yet Daddy? the big build up as he pretended to check before allowing us to run screaming with excitement into the lounge.

As children, we were brought up very strictly with a strong focus on education mingled with love in abundance, the world was often our classroom as we travelled and our school in Singapore pushed us forward, giving us confidence? It was while living in Singapore that my first Deja vu experience occurred. Dad had been on one of his trips and decided to take us to another part of Malaysia for a weekend break, our family adventures were great fun so we were thrilled. Walking along through the busy markets I stopped suddenly, if moaning was a sport I would have won Gold. Pleading in my whiniest voice was sure to do the trick, I was always happy as a rule, this would throw them off guard for sure. Do we have to climb all those steps? my legs are too tired, 'which steps darling?' said Mum clutching my hand tighter. 'The steps up the road a little bit near the monkey statue, they go to the temple in the sky '. Minutes later, sure enough we approached a huge flight of wide narrow spaced steps that seemed to go on forever, they led to a magnificent temple. The monkey statue proudly stood at the foot of the steps no doubt on duty, I had never been there in my life. It wasn't long before spiritual experiences were so normal that we had no need to mention them, Dad hadn't acknowledged them anyway so whether he believed I cannot be sure, but do you know I thought it irrelevant as he never once belittled them.

*

CHAPTER FIVE

The Mucky Beck

Wherever we lived our house was filled with laughter and lovely smells, Mum's Estee Lauder Youth Dew and Chanel no/5 filled the air on special occasions, with Soir de Paris and Californian Poppy wherever she had been at other times. I smell her perfume to this day and often catch the fragrance of Lavender polished furniture that welcomed us home. Throughout our childhood we were happy, I was later to face challenges in life that were almost unbearable, but spirit had set the pace with great preparation by saying loud and clear 'how can you understand suffering if you have never suffered?' In that moment I understood that I had been given a loving childhood with protected insight to the world of spirit in preparation for the 'bigger picture' Many things happened to me spiritually in those early years that gave immense comfort, my gratitude continues.

How about this, can you believe what a strange child I was around puberty? I would tidy graves that had been neglected, often having visits from the occupants of the graves, calling by to say thank you. We chatted happily and not knowing any different fear was never an issue. My peers played in the adjacent recreation ground, they knew exactly where I was but rather than 'outing' me as some sort of weirdo child they were gracious loyal friends, especially my bestie Elaine Aka Lainie. Funnily enough I wasn't afraid of many things but one fear that carried on into adulthood was a deep fear of dirty water as in brown flood type water. It was fear so intense that my body would shake and I would root to the spot vomiting just seeing a river about to burst its banks or television news reports showing severe floods. It was a relief to find out why in later years and you will see how I discovered the origin of that fear, also how it subsided.

Innocently, the first obvious realisation of that fear was when my brother Peter and I took a short cut into town walking alongside the beck, quite aptly called the mucky beck due to its murky brown water.

There was a large piece of pipework crossing the beck at one point, with huge coils of barbed wire across the top to prevent people from climbing onto it, although to be honest who in their right mind would want to do that? Peter jokingly said that we should cross the beck which was deep at that point, by edging along the rim of the pipe base. I was wearing new sandals and had almost caused a sword fight at dawn with Mum to be allowed this trendy style instead of the practical clod hopper type regulation sandals. Awareness of having to face an extremely angry mother if there was so much as a scuff mark was fearful. That thought turned to oh my goodness what if one slipped off and fell into the beck? then the dread kicked in, what if Peter fell into the beck how could I save him? the dirty water would swallow him up then drag me under fighting for breath as I choked on the filthy debris floating in the water. All so very irrational because Peter had no intention of crossing the beck, none of the imagined scenario would have happened. I cannot describe the sheer terror that was instilled in my head and soul, I was beside myself. Peter tried to make me laugh as we walked along the path, then we came to the bridge where the path continued underneath it but very close to the water's edge. Murky and brown the water lapped over the edge onto the path touching our feet. 'What if it floods completely Peter before we get to the other end? 'I cried, panicking and hysterical by the time we emerged safely through.

We caught the bus home, my fears seemed stupid yet nightmares of murky brown flood water swallowing me into the deepest darkest suffocating depths lasted for many years.

I love my brother Peter more than life itself and felt vulnerable for both of us. Yet this event as you will see was not the origin of my fear, however it did exacerbate the fear deeply hidden in my head.

CHAPTER SIX

Saying Goodbye To Rose Cottage

Baby Sheila our little sister, eight years younger than me came into the world along the way and was growing fast. All of us loved our house with fairy doors in the trees and in our bedroom skirting boards courtesy of our gentle fun grandad. It had a myriad of places to explore, hide or write, we have hilarious memories of Sharon calling Dad names as she ran away laughing, she was always in trouble but was great fun. A house full to the rafters with residual energy, a superb carved staircase and stained-glass windows in the front and back porches as well as on the first landing. Elegant marble fireplaces adorned the lounge and dining room, it was truly beautiful and huge so moving was very emotional. It became a Doctor Barnardo's Home because of its size and grounds, perfect! it was definitely a very happy home for children. We didn't begrudge it in the least because we were very nomadically minded having travelled such a lot. Moving was another adventure to us and knowing that our happy energy would be resounding positively throughout our old house made us happy too.

When I think back maybe that was another sign that children would play a significant part in my life, yet another link to my future work. We bid the house a fond goodbye, thanking it for our years of happiness before wishing love and happiness to everyone living there in the future. Our gardener Mr. Greenwood gave a sigh of relief as we were leaving, Sharon had worn the poor man down with her mischief and he always looked like an ancient warrior returning from battle. We all adored Mr. Greenwood. Grandma Daisy was happy, so Hello new house, we were looking forward to new experiences, new friends and continued loving family energy.

Having said goodbye to Rose Cottage it was time to say hello to the new house, we never did name it but instead affectionately referred to it as Scott-Alderson Hall.

Pushing open the gateway to our new home I once again knew that the house would make us welcome before Dad had even unlocked the door. Manners prevailed so everyone waited until Mum and Dad were in the hallway before dashing in excitedly in the race to choose bedrooms. I stood outside looking at the place we were going to trust to be our sanctuary, I drank in the brick work, the lovely wooden door and shaped step,

I smelled the flowers clambering up the wall and felt at home. An asset of being spiritually sensitive is being able to scan and absorb good energy easily with instant effect, not too good if there is negative energy around in whatever shape or form temporary or residual. No one thought it strange as I walked around touching and smelling things, they had come to terms with my little oddities. Happy that the house felt right I wandered into the garden and there it was, a long, very neglected greenhouse covered in ivy. It was on a lower level and reached by cute stone steps, love at first sight. I commandeered it without protest because it was full of creepy crawlers and looked lost. Making it my own, I spent endless happy hours in there, more often than not talking to spirit and writing or drawing. Our parents' room had pretty yellow rose chintzy wallpaper, it overlooked the garden and had fabulous energy, I loved that room. In fact, each room was tastefully decorated, stylish yet homely just waiting for Mum's artistic flair. But most of all it was this house where the story began that was to one day shape my future, a spiritual experience too profound to be ignored.

However, prior to that future experience I had been in the greenhouse drawing one day, feeling at peace with the world, we had a beautiful wood at the end of our land so everything within view was the best that nature could provide. 'Valderee Valderar', Mum was calling me for afternoon tea,

Dad was home on leave and we all had our food together chatting happily. Shortly afterwards Peter went to the cinema with friends, Mum and Dad had gone to visit our darling grandad Harold in hospital, I was earning extra pocket money by babysitting my sisters. Once they were snuggled into bed with comics and cuddlies I settled on the sofa to do some homework for school. It was growing darker outside, so I flicked on some cosy lamps around the lounge never imagining what was about to happen.

Moments later I was reading a biology book when I felt my long hair gently rising from where it rested down my back, it felt as though invisible hands were lifting it yet no one else was in the room. I felt nervous and off guard almost afraid to look around as higher and higher my hair rose, shaking with fear not daring to move wishing out loud that my parents were home, minutes seemed like hours. Unsure of how long I sat there afraid to move is uncertain and that warm cosy room had become chillingly cold. How on earth had I missed that whilst scanning the energy? That was my first negative spiritual experience and I felt out of my depth. 'What do you want with me? I called out and distinctly heard the voice of a man plaintively saying 'help me, help me ', the fear in me dissolved. The voice seemed to echo from beneath the sofa as though it was in a box really muffled. As suddenly as it had all begun, my hair was placed gently down my back again, the room was warm once more and things were normal. As you can probably imagine, it felt strange to say the least, really rocking my comfort zone, but curiously I wanted to know why this man needed help and I was no longer afraid. Back from the hospital Mum and Dad updated me on the most loving grandad ever and then I told them what had happened, knowing that Mum for sure would not dismiss it as wild imagination. Dad made a cup of tea while I related to Mum what the man had said, the words were pouring out and I was visualising an old well, Mum was fascinated wanting to know more, but there wasn't any more to know. A few days later, Mum was talking to Mrs. Ambler our fabulously gorgeous Avon lady who quite naturally asked how we were settling in. I blurted out that we loved the house but I wasn't sure about the invisible visitor. Far from thinking that we needed urgent therapy for a vivid imagination, Mrs. Ambler recounted some interesting history surrounding our house, she herself had lived in the area for a long time. It was believed that originally our house was built over a large well with a stream running beneath it, Mrs. Ambler said rumour had it that the landowner sold the land complete with the well that was undeclared. He had evidently intended to cover the hole somehow against the principles of his wife, they were arguing and the landowner fell backwards into the well too deeply to be saved. Somehow, the incident was covered up, his disappearance conveniently embellished and many years later perhaps our house was built over the concealed well or was on that same piece of land. Could the landowner have been reaching out needing his sad tale to be told or was it a modern-day Urban Myth? we will never be sure, but we built an area in the garden especially for him and said a loving goodbye, wishing him love. He never visited again and we lived there happily for several years. In fact, we were living in the same house when something happened that played a massive part in shaping my future, it centred around Grandma Jane Eleanor.

CHAPTER SEVEN

My Lavender Lady

Excruciating pain in my abdomen caused me to double up writhing on my sugar pink bedroom carpet, praying for the pain to go away. Sixteen years old by now and very afraid, my beautiful mother Hylda Adelaide Veronica (Matron) was on Palliative nursing duty visiting a patient whose life was drawing to an end. Mum chose to work she was a nurturer, a true earth angel where nursing was a vocation never just a job, she had risen rapidly through the ranks to become a highly respected Matron. Not doing the RAF overseas postings any more due to our further education, Mum became devoted and passionate about helping anyone suffering the burden of illness. We loved her even more because of it and she was always my inspiration. It was 7 pm, I could hear the clock ticking hypnotically, sound magnified, trying to focus on the regular beat in a vain attempt to divert from the pain. Grabbing the nearest receptacle which just happened to be a pretty lace trimmed waste bin, I was violently sick, wet and trembling from the perspiration soaking my long fair hair and clothes. Never having experienced pain like it fear shuddered through my whole being but I couldn't call out for Dad who was downstairs oblivious to my distress. Based overseas as he was at the time with his RAF Squadron he had recently returned home on leave, this unexpected event would surely freak him out.

Dad was quietly enjoying the lounge to himself reading his newspaper in peace, Sharon and Sheila were snuggled up along the landing from my room, they loved their bedtime and were sleeping soundly. Both blissfully unaware of the distress a few rooms away thank goodness. Peter was overseas having followed in Dad's career footsteps.

Not wanting anyone to worry about me I tried desperately to stifle the agonising groans emanating as the pain increased. Downstairs Dad heard Tiger the family cat scratching outside the lounge door, he sighed loudly then stretched ready to stand up and let her in. Being a total man's man Dad cherished his little bit of 'boy' time and begrudgingly opened the door for Tiger. As he did so he heard a low groaning sound from upstairs, his senses were on high alert one of his chicklets was in trouble.

Anything to escape the pain I had banged my head on the skirting along the wall in a frenzied attempt to knock myself out. The girls slept on, Dad had raced upstairs his primal instincts fuelled by an Adrenaline rush drawn by the raw urgency in the sounds. Heart pounding Dad effortlessly lifted me his eldest daughter up and carried me downstairs wrapped in my Quilted bedspread. His fear was palpable, two of my sisters had passed as babies, he knew that raw grief. Barely conscious I struggled to recognise where I was, infection raged through my body, my temperature soared sky high. 'Mummy please help me it hurts so badly', I cried on hearing my mother's gentle voice and feeling her soft hand on my forehead. A thermometer was popped into my mouth as someone rapped sharply on the front door. Mum hadn't even taken her coat off when her old school friend, our family doctor walked in all 'Jolly hockey sticks dahhlings' Doctor Moody took one look at me, gently pressed my abdomen and immediately phoned for an ambulance. 'Appendicitis! get here quickly! Waste no time at all', her voice commanded before giving our address.

The ambulance crew adeptly loaded their precious cargo onto the ambulance, one monitoring observations as he placed a metal kidney dish on to my chest, the other driving urgently to the Royal Infirmary. I laugh to myself now remembering how old fashioned the vehicles, equipment and crews were back then, in sharp contrast to the state-of-the art medical equipment, computerised systems, satellite navigation radios and vehicles I have worked with.

Mum and Doctor Moody sat opposite the stretcher bed, their expressions showing deep concern, Mum stroked her 'lucky' rabbits foot brooch adorned with an amethyst stone for good luck. Sensing the two women and the ambulance man watching me I suddenly realised that the pain had gone, it had completely disappeared, the guilt was overwhelming, the shame, no better than a fraudster. Pondering what I should do, eyes tightly closed fearful of being caught out in a lie, Ambulance speeding along, bells clanging away what will happen?

Being transferred from the stretcher trolley onto a sheet of coarse hospital green paper towelling felt cold and impersonal, it covered a yukky brown examination couch. It was in the Emergency department at the Royal Infirmary, my eyes opened to sighs of relief all around me. Pink with embarrassment after a bunch of very personal examinations and tests I was wheeled onto a ward where the screens were promptly pulled to encompass my bed. Mum was sent to have a cup of tea, lost and lonely in the crisp stiffly laundered sheets I wanted my Mum so much but at sixteen needed to be at least a little bit grown up. Returning to kiss her poorly daughter goodnight, Mum was about to leave having been told by the ward Sister to go home and rest, it was no longer an emergency, mothers therefore were surplus to requirements.

Suddenly the sound of a stretcher trolley being pushed at high speed broke the silence of the night my screens were flung open without ceremony or explanation. By then the pain which had slowly been niggling again was building up to a crescendo and the nausea had come back. My words were barely audible as I tried to tell the staff, their concern was palpable as they transferred me at speed onto the trolley. No words of reassurance, no loving hugs or comforting smiles just an overwhelming sense of urgency. Ceiling lights above the pale blue painted corridors whizzed by in a blur, I felt light headed wanting to sleep and not wake up. Voices in the distance 'sharp scratch Valerie 'said one of them, a horrible smelling black rubber mask went over my face, was that before they crashed through the green theatre doors or after? I was past caring the pain was bad again. Faces partly hidden by Sherwood green theatre masks and caps hovered above me then disappeared to be replaced by a wonderful sea of darkness. *I Am Me, No One Special*. Where am I and why is no one here straining to focus on my surroundings I tried to lift my head from the bed, but it felt weird and heavy. A faint glow a little way in front sought my attention, I stared beyond it, wondering could anyone else see what I could, no shape or colour, very strange. Dainty footsteps echoed, I heard the lady approach before seeing her, sensing that she was there for me but not having a clue who she was. When the visitor sat on the bed it felt natural, she silently held my hand and time was irrelevant. A soothing scent of lavender cologne wafted in the air around the bed as if to announce her presence. Absorbing every detail of the lady who carried herself in old fashioned elegance I found her presence comforting, she had an aura of tranquillity and I gazed in awe at the beautiful face in front of me I wanted to capture everything.

Glossy auburn tinted brown hair framed my visitor's face, it was cut short with a long fringe swept to the right in a classic Marcelle wave. The other side styled to tuck behind her left ear, a tiny pearl earring was exposed and again the lavender fragrance filled the air lingering softly. A cream blouse with fine crochet type collar and pearl buttons was all but covered by a fine knit long brown cardigan with matching tailored skirt. Completing her outfit, she wore shiny bootee type shoes with tiny side buttons. 'Valerie everyone thinks that you are going to die but you still have far too much to do, it is not time for you to go yet. You will look after many children in a foreign country, your calling is to be their mother and love them as your own. That will be your life's work and I will walk beside you'. The words were spoken softly and didn't make any sense, yet I experienced a powerful aura of freedom and relief. Leaning over, the Lavender Lady kissed my forehead before brushing a stray lock of hair from near to her left eye, then she turned and walked back towards the glow. As the glow dissipated slowly, once more I sank into the twilight world of my temporary home, a world of darkness unaware of the time, day and night were the same it made not one iota of difference to me. In Twilight world, it was dreamlike and peaceful, the darkness welcomed my Lavender Lady, it was a happy feeling. After one visit, she held my hand as usual then said firmly ' Valerie, you will hear laughter and feel that laughter in your soul. That is the day that you will start to live your life' again, she said that she would always walk beside me, it was her last visit. Three weeks had passed when I eventually emerged from my twilight world of coma, unaware of how close to death I had been, that last rites had been read at my bedside. My Appendix had burst, poisoning my body almost shutting it down, intensive care had been home for a little while, the tubes had been removed and I was moved to a small 4 bed ward, breathing unaided though still very poorly. A police officer's wife was opposite, she was recovering from surgery her name was Valerie Overton. In pain and sleeping my eyes were closed then Valerie began to laugh out loud and I started to laugh too. Within minutes my eyes were wide open and focusing, everyone seemed elated.

CHAPTER EIGHT

Grandma Jane Eleanor

Sitting on my pixie pouffe I reflected as I looked around the family lounge, two weeks convalescence in the cottage hospital had seemed endless. It was good to be home but there was no getting away from the questions that niggled. 'why didn't anyone visit me in the big hospital?' I asked tossing the dice onto my sister's snakes and ladders board, the question was directed at family. I sat petulantly waiting for a list of excuses as to why they had neglected me for three whole weeks, talk about self-centred drama queen I surely deserved the me me me crown. Okay, they said that I was unconscious but where is the logic, how could I be wide awake for the Lavender Lady but not for family? it just did not make sense. Mum looked up from her embroidery sporting the 'kind Mum' bemused smile as she gently explained how everything was touch and go so someone was with me twenty-four hours a day, the adult family members had all been beside the bed in relays.

Sharon piped up with 'tell Mummy about the lady Valerie', 'which lady darling?' Mum asked genuinely curious. Hesitating for a moment, had delirium controlled those weeks of darkness, would everyone question my sanity? 'Oh! no one,' I said defensively, 'well just my Lavender Lady'. Seeing the look on Mum's face was worrying as the experience unravelled bit by bit revealing details of the gentle lady who had given loving comfort through the whole ordeal. Mum paled significantly before fainting in front of us, 'please don't be poorly Mummy' said Sheila and burst into tears. Dad rushed to help Mum, he made her comfortable on the sofa then ensuring that she was fully recovered and sipping her cup of tea he went up to the attic.

Minutes later Dad returned holding a Decoupage lacquered box, unlocking the box he asked me to look through it without saying why. 'Mummy look!!!! 'I shrieked as I shuffled the old sepia brown photos, 'it's my Lavender Lady, it is really her look everyone' I waved the photo aloft joyfully, she was exactly as I had seen her in hospital. It was Grandma Jane Eleanor (Jinny to Grandad Harold), she was my mother's very own dearly loved mother. Grandma had passed when Mum, her precious much-loved daughter was only thirteen years of age, so very tragic. Mum had held onto the tremendous grief of her mother's loss silently, it had broken her heart and was too painful to talk to any of us about, it was a very sad feeling hearing that. Our Mum was all that a mother could possibly be and even more, so knowing that she had such a lot of pain was awful. Grandma Jane had obviously returned to watch over her only daughters' child. Wanting a daughter desperately, Grandma Jane had marked Mum's birth by wearing a dainty pearl earring on her left ear. She used to tuck a piece of lint soaked in lavender cologne for headache pain. As we talked lovingly about Grandmas visits in hospital all of us had a strong psychic breeze flowing over us and we smelled a fresh lavender fragrance. Mum had released her grief and we knew that we would get to hear more about Grandma. Grandma Janes prediction for my future was to come true about caring for children overseas, it was to become bigger than I ever could imagine.

A few days later we were talking about what Grandma Jane had said regarding children, Mum reminded me of a Conversation we had when flying back to the UK from Singapore. We had landed in India, the aircraft was on the apron, some people had reached their destination, they had disembarked. Others were boarding, overhead lockers were opened and closed, passengers chatted, cabin crew organised, flight deck tannoi messages reverberated, it was all going on. Oblivious to all of it I watched barefooted urchins pulling at the clothes of transiting passengers, they were begging for rupees or American dollars. Heat vapour was rising from the scorching tarmac, I worried about their dear little feet and felt tears rolling down my cheeks, we had such a happy life it was unfair.

Mum told me that the children were mostly orphans without anyone to care for them, I was a child but looked into her turquoise blue eyes and stated with full conviction 'one day I will come back to India and look after the children'. It came from my heart and I meant it, Mum looked at me, her eyes full of love as she spoke gently 'you will darling, you will'.

CHAPTER NINE

Daffodils for Anne

As a young divorced Mum, I moved to Essex with my son Jason aged four and soon built up a close network of friends. One of those friends was Anne, she had a little boy at the toddler stage and had recently given birth to another dear little boy. Anne and her boys were doted on by her husband, he was happily in the process of turning their cosy house into a dream family home. Anne was a natural mother and a loving friend, we enjoyed and valued our coffee morning chats, never running out of things to say. Suffering from severe asthma Anne refused to allow it to affect her life, she had so many plans for her future. When Anne chatted to someone new her shyness showed clearly, she would stand head to one side twiddling long strands of shiny brown hair in her fingers whilst rubbing her right foot behind her left leg at the same time. I had been to London for the weekend and was excited to be seeing Anne for a catch up over coffee, she had been making things for the playroom and was keen to show me. Smiling at first when I saw a neighbour near my car, then becoming concerned when she said in an unusually strange tone 'where are you going Valerie?' Having already spent hours trying to stave off a horrible feeling of apprehension my stomach flipped. 'Anne's house for coffee' I replied 'why?' 'Oh, Valerie dear I am so very sorry to tell you this, but your friend Anne died yesterday' the scream was delayed 'Nooooo!!!! She can't be dead' I cried then jumped into my car. Margaret held onto the handle to prevent me from driving off, I drove on auto pilot reaction to Anne's house at the far end of the village and ran towards the door. It opened, Anne's husband had been pre-warned by Margaret, he met me in the drive and we held each other as we cried together for the damned unfairness of it all.

Asthma had got the better of her in the end, it had happened so fast and the three people who loved her as much as was possible to love anyone had lost her in minutes, my loss as painful as it was seemed miniscule compared to theirs. Funeral day arrived, the church service though beautiful was distressing beyond words, I was so open to multiple spirits wanting to talk to me, not having protected myself it was just too difficult at that time. Learning to cope with funerals was on my 'To do' list.

Anne was due to be buried that day in the village churchyard but the ground that harsh winter was too solid, it caused horrendous additional distress to family and friends. The poor vicar was distraught having watched Anne grow up into the lovely woman she had become, doing her wedding service and the two christening services as highlights during that time. For weeks I cried worrying about Anne's children and how sad their world would be without her and how much she would miss out on.

As spring arrived I can remember seeing the churchyard full of bright sunshiny yellow daffodils, I sat in the car bawling my eyes out thinking, Anne would have loved the daffodils they were one of her favourite flowers because they heralded the spring, her most looked forward to season. Weeks went by in a blur, work was robotic, and sadness pervaded my life, I had survivor guilt and only functioned by pretending to be alright. Being blessed with a darling son who had already been through too much this was his loss as well, he needed to acknowledge his pain, so I had to be strong for him.

One day three of my friends turned up, bundling me into a car with them, my protests were ignored as they drove me to a magnificent place not far from Stansted airport, Stansted Hall. Never having been there before I must have looked like a rabbit trapped in headlights, I had absolutely no idea where the heck we were.

Two middle aged ladies welcomed us and as they looked at me whispered 'you're one of us dear, aren't you?' 'OMG they think that I'm a lesbian' I said to my friends, they giggled. I didn't bat an eyelid as some of the best people in my life are gay and gorgeous. Sitting in the seats we were guided to, in what appeared to be a quaint little chapel I looked around curious as to why they had taken me there. 'Oh, my goodness there are three healers here, can you see them?' I asked the girls, 'no' they said in unison. Pointing to two people a few rows in front of us then to a third person a couple of rows down on our right, I explained what made them different to anyone else. The palest of blue auras were around each of them, a little shield of lovely healing energy. Patently clear to me but invisible to the girls, it is so simple to assume that everyone can 'see' but also frustrating when they would love to see into my world, a world I would love to share.

Music started, a soothing hymn, then a Scottish sounding lady introduced herself as a Spiritual Medium before pointing out the three healers I had spotted, who were in fact guest Mediums.

Fascinated, I listened as messages were given out to appreciative members of the congregation from loved ones that have passed, not concerned about a message for myself in the least. Instead happy for everyone else I realised that dear friends had kindly sought solace for me in a place they knew would be perfect, my gratitude knew no bounds. Following the service, we joined the rest of the visitors in a room where refreshments were being served, books lined the shelves and one of the two Mediums manning the door on our arrival asked me to find two books for her. Immediately, the books found me, practically jumping out I was drawn to the shelves they were on, but before I could hand the books to her she stood with her head to one side, fiddling with her hair she rubbed her right leg behind her left leg. 'Anne said thank you for thinking of her with great love when you saw the daffodils', the friends I was with and I burst into tears, Anne's passing to a wonderful higher life was validated and we each knew then that she was happy.

From then onwards I was able to accept Anne's passing, her wish it seems was for her husband to remarry, this he did eventually to a gracious, happy soul, a fantastic mother to his boys.

God bless caring friends and the loving power of spirit. Following that comforting experience, I researched Stansted Hall or Arthur Findlay College as it is now, and it is renowned for psychic sciences, spiritual development and healing for those who attend for studies, teaching courses or for rest time. The Hall was built in 1871 and the college was founded in 1964 a year after his wife's death, when in accordance to Arthur Findlay's wishes, the Hall, grounds and endowment were transferred to The Spiritualists National Union. He left for Higher life aged 81 on July 24th1964, and the college goes from strength to strength, people attend from all over the world. Of course, it has even more to offer now in the way of Spiritual development and although I have been back there a few times I would love the time to visit more often.

CHAPTER TEN

None of us are perfect

Early months following my divorce were very painful and exceptionally traumatic, I left behind a lovely home and practically all my treasured belongings but most of all the man that I had married, and thought would be my forever man. My ex-husband kindly said that he is happy for me to talk about that time in our life because he has turned his life around in many ways and we have over the years maintained a good family friendship, all of us love and care about him very much. He is still basically a kind, generous man with a heart of gold and would help anyone, not many people are aware, but he is a very talented musician and if 'life' hadn't got in the way he would probably be out there on a par with the great musicians of that time.

During that awful time when we were young I was escaping from a husband who loved me like a princess, buying extravagant jewellery, designer clothes and other gifts, leaving because part of his personality was very flawed. None of us are perfect, I have many flaws, but his flaws were damaging, and no number of presents could compensate for the cruelty he unknowingly imposed at times when his illness took hold. I hasten to add that it was chemically induced behaviour that mimicked schizophrenia. Yet on good days he placed me on a pedestal sky high, we had a lot of laughter on those days. Doctors ignored my pleas, I tried so hard to get help for him everywhere including Harley street, but he is the first to admit that he didn't want help then. We were almost set up for failure even though on the surface as a couple we had it all. Over the years we have talked about that time and I am truly proud of him because he never denies it or backs away from taking responsibility, he is a good person who had health related problems at the time. Our divorce was settled in the High Court of London due to the severity of events, it was a very sad day for both of us.

Over the years once the initial bitterness had been too energy consuming to hold on to we began to stay in touch, keeping each other updated on life, my happiest time was when his medication gave him hope. Bless his heart he is so remorseful when he looks back but has encouraged my writing 100% and I thank him sincerely because had we not gone through those times I may never have been strong enough to do the work I do. Remaining close to the family matters because how could I divorce a family that welcomed me lovingly like their own flesh and blood? I have wonderfully happy memories to be grateful for.

Financially it was awful having left everything of value and worth behind including my house. Someone was collecting me from hospital on the day I left so my husband had gone off to a tattoo parlour to have mine and our sons name drawn onto his arm. He had hoped that all would be well, but his uncle had arrived to drive my son and I to Essex, no turning back. It had been fabulous living in Middlesex, bumping willy nilly into celebrities almost every time I shopped (my very impressionable days of course).

Goodbye Middlesex thank you for a lovely stay. Finding it too painful for any attachment or gain from the sale of our lovely home etc. I walked away with nothing even though it would have set my financial security solidly.

CHAPTER ELEVEN

When Karma Bites, It Bites Hard

Hello Essex, here we are.

We stayed with Mum and Dad who reverted to be the parents of teenagers again, they were hilariously strict. My sisters and I had loads of fun just looking at the steps Dad took to catch us out if we were late home, late for him was arriving home from the cinema at 10-30 pm on a Saturday night. Sheila got away with anything, she was the ultimate Daddy's girl, she could be out all night with friends and when asked where she had been would smile cutely and say that she had been strawberry picking. I had the equivalent of the Spanish inquisition if I was out past 10-00 pm. Sharon didn't care, she was impervious to any hints of fatherly sarcasm and would make it her mission to set us off laughing. Poor Dad, a long career in the RAF had not prepared him for the wiles of three daughters, we loved him so much. Had I stayed there for more than a few weeks the poor man would have gone crackers, so I planned and decided. One day I took the plunge borrowed a map book and stuck a pin in a page covering Essex.

Two weeks later we were settled in a chocolate box village, welcomed and accepted by everyone, it quickly became home. That bit of background is to show you how life is made up of peaks and troughs, it is how we deal with them that matters. Also, how karma really does come back big time to bite people on the bottom. This is one example and karma doesn't often bite harder than this, see what you think. Not long after moving to the village I needed to buy another car to replace our temporary hire car having left my own in Middlesex. As luck would have it (or not, as it turned out), there was a small garage not too far from us and had cars for sale on its forecourt. Off I trotted, cash in hand with my son eagerly beside me, he pointed to a turquoise blue 'girly' mobile 'Mummy you love that colour' he said excitedly and jumped into the driver's seat.

A rather chunky man headed towards us, he made a fuss of my son before reeling out the remarkable features and virtues of the seemingly prince of cars, adding that it was ridiculously economical.

Explaining my situation to him it left him in no uncertain terms that the car would have to be reliable as high breakdown expense at that time was out of the question. A safe reliable car was vital because it would be carrying something more precious than anything, my son. He and I had been through so much together with still a long road to travel. The car salesman was all charm or was that smarm? As he extolled the wealth of positives that pretty blue car had to offer. Papers signed, money handed over, handshake, ignition turned and off we drove happy as anything. As a young mum determined to survive for my son it almost felt that things really could only get better, where on earth was the psychic instinct warning me, was it a case of being desperate to trust someone? Less than one mile away from the garage black smoke billowed from the engine, the car ground to a halt, my son cried, and I felt sick as my heart lurched with the realisation that someone evil had duped me.

An off-duty fireman stopped to help, he was also a qualified mechanic and looked over the car 'so sorry sweetheart' he said as he placed his arm comfortingly around my shoulder. 'The engine is knackered, whoever sold this to you knew exactly what he was doing and let you buy it complete with its duff engine and other related problems.' After offering to go to the garage with his mates and give him a knuckle sandwich on my behalf, he left his phone number in case it seemed like a good proposition. Believe me the temptation was almost too much. I phoned the garage asking to speak to the owner, surprise! surprise! it was smarmy man himself who just laughed, not one ounce of remorse, empathy or conscience. In those days the legal system didn't always cater for such situations, blue car had so much wrong with her (yes, I know, but to me she was a girl car) that it could only be throwing money away to have her fixed, lots of money lost or cheated out of, hard lessons learned for future reference. Finding where the garage owner lived was easy, he boasted about his home and lifestyle so much that people knew where he lived. The trappings of his wealth were on show for all to see and envy, his sailing boat on a flash trailer in front of the house and brand new luxury 'his' hers' and 'the kids' cars, mountain bikes etc adorned the drive. Envy was the last emotion in my heart, who could ever wish to be like that cold, calculating excuse for a human being. Proudly walking up his drive, head held high I faced him unafraid, 'look at my child's face and mine because I am certain that when Karma bites your bottom one of us will witness your downfall'. Not raising my voice, staying strong and proud, I continued fully aware that other people had gathered around.' When you walk a mile in someone else's shoes you may have a little humility, right now I feel sorry for you. Huh! Look at everything I've got, don't feel sorry for me feel jealous'. In a lightbulb moment any bitterness I had felt towards him vanished, he was a greedy man not a happy man, my happiness was deliriously so by comparison. Walking back down his drive, I looked at his massive house, his swimming pool, his three children on expensive motor cycles and the flashy cars. Thank you, my angels for giving me insight into that man's soul, thank goodness he sold the car to me and not someone unable to cope.

Years later I was in the ambulance service working one day with my pal Fred, we were sent to pick a chap up from a rather dubious block of flats in a not too affluent part of town. It was given to us as a U case (GP referral as urgent but not an emergency). Control staff advised us that the chap lived alone and was a double leg amputee with ulcerated infected stumps. Fred and I were determined to really nurture the poor man and ensure that his journey was really comfortable. Crews from our station were known for giving excellent care but it just came as second nature to practically all of us. We were certain that our patient would be feeling very poorly so we had planned on the journey there how to carry out our various transfers in the least traumatic way.

Arriving at the block of flats we grabbed our equipment, heading for the lift to his flat four floors up. The lift stank of urine, discarded take away food cartons were strewn everywhere leaving a vile smell of stale onions. In the corridor conditions were no better, all we could smell was used wet nappies that strong ammonia smell of dehydration. We really felt for the poor chap we were collecting, wanting so much to make his life better.

Knocking at the door we heard 'come in door's open' pushing the door wide enough to fit our equipment and stretcher trolley Fred and I greeted the man with a cheery 'hello there' he replied with a more sombre version, understandably. 'BANG!!!!! Imaginary fireworks going off in my head, I remained calm, my face not showing an incy bit of emotion breathe Valerie breathe! he hasn't recognised you, you're a professional, keep calm I told myself. My heart raced as I tried to behave with some sort of normality. Lowering my voice, I stated 'this is Fred, I am Susan', Fred looked over but knew me well enough to go with the flow, that there would be a good reason. Our eyes looked around the hovel of a flat before I dare focus on the patient again, phew!! he still hadn't recognised me.

'There let's make you comfy, and before we take you to hospital we can clean your commode, water your plants then empty your bins so that the flat will be fresh to come home to. The chap kept thanking me, Fred glanced at me with raised eyebrows so while watering the plants I scribbled a note. OMG Fred he is the evil car man I told you about, please humour me and follow my lead. Fred knew that my nurturing would be genuine and that whatever this man had done I would never hurt him, jeopardise professionalism or forfeit our strict duty of care conduct code. We treated our patient like a precious gem, where were his trappings of wealth now? his flat was filthy barely furnished no obvious luxury items anywhere, how the mighty had fallen.

Still not recognising me he poured his heart out on the journey to hospital, Fred had swapped with me so that he drove, and I could attend our patient, but Fred could hear our conversation. Eager to bend sympathetic ears the chap told us that he had lost his home, wife and children, cars, boat and business due to bad investments and gambling. Holding our attention he continued by telling us that without his money he had nothing to offer, they wanted money not him. Living such a rich life had been unhealthy, he developed severe gout and diabetes stole the health of his legs, gangrene left no alternative other than to amputate. Making appropriate sounds in response to his story we listened as he told us that their friends had all snubbed him so there wasn't a soul to care about him. Arriving at the hospital we handed him over to admission staff with his notes. He thanked us for our help, I looked into his still cold unfeeling eyes knowing that he was still only concerned with himself, understandable with good reason to now. 'Fred and I are sad that you are suffering and hope that you can be made as comfortable as possible', I said quietly. In the same tone of voice without raising it 'my real name is Valerie, I bought a bought a pretty blue car from you for my little boy and I', no need really to say more, his expression said it all, but it could not be left in limbo,

'God pays debts in mysterious ways and I have seen Karma bite you hard as predicted', I carried on, 'that said, I wish you well because I was taught to love not hate'. Finally, I had closure for my son and I, does that make me a bad person?

He sadly passed a few months later with only hospital staff attending his funeral.

CHAPTER TWELVE

Daphne I'm Having Twins

Going back to the sad heartbreak of losing Anne, shortly after that episode of events I met someone who was great fun. Born to elderly parents and growing up in a more mature environment he was a very adult nineteen - year old. He'd worked in London pubs bottling up and sorting beer barrels etc being too young to do bar work when he started. With a huge extended family of aunties, uncles, cousins, nephews, nieces and grandparents who adored him, getting together was fun. Friends all seemed older than him and I always felt that he was waiting for a childhood that never came, he was a man at sixteen and at the age of nineteen was confident and popular. Caring and kind, my son Jason adopted him as a big brother figure after my sister Sheila introduced us. Sheila was working with him, our parents knew him therefore it was natural progression for our friendship to grow into a relationship. In 1981 we were blessed with our beautiful twins Luke (Pooky) and Zoe (Zozzie) whom we adored. With Jason as their fabulous big brother all was good.

My family in spirit had told me that twin babies were coming and engaged with me during a very difficult pregnancy. I knew that I was pregnant within days of conception before nature even gave me a useful hint in that direction. My friend Daphne had invited me to her house a few miles away and it was wonderful being there the spiritual energy was in abundance. 'Daphne! I am having a boy and girl twins', 'but you don't even look pregnant, how far on are you? It's so exciting' she exclaimed hugging me tightly. 'Oh! I haven't done a test yet' was my response, 'Grandad Harold Kelly Alderson in spirit told me and he never once lied to me'. Being very spiritual herself Daphne completely 'got it' and was happy. We walked to nearby shops where there was an old - fashioned florist shop, it had the cutest hand painted cardboard egg in the window. Near to it were two tiny dolls one dressed in pink, the other in blue, we entered the shop and gently picking up the egg I opened it. Placing the dolls in each half of the egg I smiled at Daphne then bought them. To this day the eggs and the dolls live with me and are treasured as much as the day they were bought. A few weeks later Daphne and I waited eagerly for the pregnancy test results knowing they would be positive, Daphne had never doubted. It was fun chatting with Daphne about the spiritual activity in her home and we often walked around the house seeing what energy we would pick up. One day that stuck in my mind was when we both felt the need to tip toe quietly along the landing, it seemed important. 'Daphne a child was very poorly in that room with a dangerously high temperature' they put straw on the road to prevent the horse's hooves from clattering when the milk was delivered', it was comfortable relating to my friend because she too saw the things I did. Ray and Daphne's lovely old house with its many secret doorways and passages had masses of residual energy, it was wonderful spending time there, their love and friendship are still truly valued to this day. They live near the sea now which I feel is good for them but the selfish me misses them very much.

The early days of my pregnancy seemed to drag endlessly yet my tummy was growing at a rate of knots, at twelve weeks the already huge bump was scanned confirming indeed that the stork would be delivering twinlets to our house, Yippee! Geronimo! For someone who loves children and could never imagine life without them it was just the most wonderful news ever, not the least bit daunting. My parents seemed to have a new lease of life on hearing the scan results and wanted me to spend as much time with them as possible. I suffered from Hyperemesis badly through almost all my pregnancy and was unable to tolerate food of any kind, even fluids made me vomit from morning to night. My darling Mummy gave me vitamin and iron injections daily, reassuring me and monitoring the babies constantly.

Heading to their home one morning I let myself in and noticed tea cups abandoned full of cold tea, their bed was unmade, and my parents were nowhere to be seen, in a moment of realisation that all was not well I had a clear vision of Dad wired up to equipment fighting for his life. Knowing they would never leave the house less than immaculate, an unmade bed was not an option, my senses were on high alert. Phoning their doctor, his name Doctor Death (I know! Quite ominous but pronounced De-arth) and asked him if my Dad had suffered a CVA (cardio vascular accident or in short, a stroke) Dr, Death ahem! De-arth confirmed my worry saying that he had tried to phone me at home. The mobile I had was like a house brick so had been left at home. My Dad was seriously ill on life support, his recovery took time and my mother was truly amazing with him, we believe that she kept him alive. Paralysed, unable to speak, that wonderful man so full of the funniest quick wit, who by his charismatic presence had commanded huge respect both in his uniformed and civilian roles. It was truly heart breaking but as a family we encouraged his humour, loving nothing more than making him laugh. Mum did daily physio and speech therapy with Dad and his finest moment came when he wrote one word in large letters across a small therapy whiteboard, it made us laugh for days. They had a caring but nosey neighbour always desperate to know what was going on. One day she had timed her visit as usual to coincide with the family visit and subsequently joined us for afternoon tea as a welcome guest. She talked none stop and we were intrigued to see Dad turn away as he made every effort to write legibly on his whiteboard. Where Dad was seated, their neighbour had her back to him and with hardly any struggle for once Dad lifted the board allowing us to see it but not the neighbour. In large letters with an arrow pointing to her was the word 'Jaws'. We knew for sure then that whatever else the stroke had stolen it certainly wasn't his sense of humour.

CHAPTER THIRTEEN

Hi Ho, Hi Ho It's Back To Work I Go

Once the twins were settled into a good routine it was time to get back to my agency medical shifts on night duty, reluctant to leave them even for a minute I bit the bullet. Some of the first shifts were at St. Mary's hospital in Colchester, most of the hospitals in and around Colchester are steeped in history, St. Mary's was no exception. Originally built as the union work house for sick, destitute and aged paupers its status pre-1948 covered general care until post 1948 it became an **NHS** acute unit.

There had been so many cases over the years of smallpox, typhoid and cholera that the buildings were deemed inadequate. However, as it was the only refuge for infectious diseases it was agreed many years previously in 1860 that non pauper women suffering from venereal disease could be treated there as well. Their treatment would be carried out in a building behind the work house. A year later it was vetoed by the authorities sadly, but an area existed within the hospital that was called a 'foul ward', by 1868 this was crowded. Can you imagine the amount of suffering, indignity and death over the years? it is difficult to comprehend such terrible conditions. They certainly left behind huge imprints of residual energy that as an Empath I picked up on strongly in each hospital the agency sent me to.

If you are not historically minded then a long drawn out list of changes, dates and building additions will be of little interest to you, but take my word there are many. Provision was made for extra beds, numerous chronically sick, acute medical and not as acute medical patients had been cared for. The idea by then of St. Mary's as a public assistance institution was regarded as a thing of the past. Residual energy stayed.

That energy was packed into every fibre of the building, emanating from each brick almost palpable to someone as sensitive as an Empath.

By 1968 the hospital had been hugely modernised with wide ranging facilities and in 1985 a stroke unit was provided. I also covered a few shifts later during the stroke unit years doing a few night shifts there, experiencing how tangible the energy was. Following some shifts, I would drive home crying not for the dear vulnerable stroke patients but for the souls of the thousands of patients of years gone by. Sadness invaded my heart, but it fuelled the desire to give 100% loving, positive medical care to everyone.

The first time I saw 'him' though was before the Stroke Unit days, it was about 01-45 I had been to the sluice room and was walking back to the ward. Approaching one of the side rooms a young soldier came towards me and without speaking took off his cap, rolled it up tucking it into his epaulette. He smiled showing off wonky teeth with a cheeky grin, winked then walked into the side room. It wasn't too strange seeing someone at that unearthly hour as some patients on the unit had limited life expectancy, so relatives would hold vigil through the night.

During handover in the morning one of the staffs, said 'sadly Walter died in the night about 01-45, he has no family to our knowledge, so he can be laid out (that process is nowadays called 'Last Offices') ready for removal to the mortuary', the soldier was never mentioned.

It was two weeks later when the soldier next appeared, he was just leaving the unit I was working on. Concerned that one of my patients was cold I had collected a blanket from the linen room and was returning to the unit. This time, I said hello to the soldier who didn't speak but took the cap from his epaulette squidging it onto his head, again he smiled and winked. Checking the patients, all were sleeping so peacefully and the air was filled with tranquil energy. Margaret had passed in the short time I had been gone, kissing her on the cheek, time of death noted I drew up her personal folder for any possible contacts. Like Walter, Margaret was without family, I beeped the on call doctor to certify her death then lovingly removed all of the medical paraphernalia. Carrying out last offices was my final loving duty of care for a darling little lady.

At handover, it seemed like good protocol to mention the soldier, he could have so easily been a thief masquerading as a soldier, or God forbid someone capable of 'bumping' someone off for whatever warped reason.

'You jammy thing! I am so bloody jealous' said one of the physios, 'I would give anything to see him', then realising the significance of his statement tried to back pedal furiously. Evidently each time the soldier had appeared, the patient he had been spotted near to died. The soldier was so clear and solid in every detail, so it hadn't occurred to me that he could have been a spiritual visitor, he had certainly been seen many times before. It was only when little Edie passed that it really hit me what the soldier was, he walked through a solid kitchen wall in front of me but still managed a cheeky wink before he left.

Colchester is a very military place, so other staff and visitors had never queried his presence, what an experience yet it was never frightening, his presence was probably very soothing to people like Walter, Margaret and Edie alone in the world. One of the staff told me that a soldier had been seen offering cigarettes to patients prior to death something soldiers in battle did to provide comfort to wounded comrades. Absolutely fascinating, the hospital rippled with energy. Once the District General opened, St. Mary's became a Geriatric focused hospital only to close completely in 1993, the eleven or so shifts I covered there made me appreciate how much we must value life and the life of those we love. We can never take one second of our life on earth for granted because it can be extinguished without a moment's notice. One thing that working in the Medical and Clinical Psychology profession has taught me is how extremely fragile life can be. Also, how the healthiest person can be killed in a road traffic incident with barely a mark on them or the vehicle, yet someone else who has vulnerable health and stature can survive the most serious of accidents where a vehicle is mangled beyond recognition. No rhyme or reason.

CHAPTER FOURTEEN

Ding Dong Bell, Can You Find Our Well?

Around that time some friends invited me to afternoon tea in a quaint vintage themed Essex tea shop. They were chatting away happily, it was lovely listening to them talking about life in general, it was relaxing, we ladies were content and grateful for each bit of the day so far. A very attractive young woman approached requesting to speak to me, she was apologetic, we invited her to join us for tea and cake. Please could I visit her house as her husband wanted to find the well they knew was on their property. The craziness of life meant that this wasn't the first unusual request I had been approached with. It was then a matter of sorting dates in our diaries and me being honest as to whether my ability would stretch to finding their well, no promises. Two days later Leigh and David as I will name them for my story, greeted me with great warmth on their cobbled drive. Standing fixed for a moment my gaze was drawn down the drive to a building at the back of the house left hand side. A feeling of intense nausea washed over me, squealing sounds, chopping, the smell of blood it was awful. Leigh and David were worried but genuinely appeared oblivious to what was having such an emotional and physical effect. We had soft drinks in their beautiful garden, the negative feelings had disappeared almost immediately, and David told me that their house was steeped in history. David had been told about the presence of a well but after many searches it had remained elusive, despite research and physical help of friends. Leigh told me that David wanted to write a journal logging details and photos of the changes made prior to their arrival. It was important to him for the character of the house not to be lost completely knowing that eventually it would be in someone else's hands. It would be a hand down journal for future owners, it seemed the well was crucial to his plans. My brain was ticking over wondering whether dowsing would have been a better idea and how had I landed in this situation? Honestly, I am my own worst enemy at times. Now then finding the well was the plan of action, was it curiosity or ego that had called? I prayed that it wasn't ego because ego when working with spirit is like a whole bunch of nasty verrucae very unwelcome. Left alone to concentrate, fabulous! A good chance to talk to spirit and the loving angels forever guiding us, I asked for help then wandered around the large garden, it was definitely a show exhibit contender truly stunning, a joy to spend time in. Lost in the sheer beauty and peace, free to stroll through the vast array of flowers I was drawn to a grey stone raised ornamental flower bed, the floral displays obviously chosen for their exotic scents. Attempting to identify different plant species (you were impressed for a second, then weren't you? but to be honest I didn't have the foggiest idea) I sat on the edge around the flower bed which was wide enough to sit reasonably comfortably though I was still grateful for my well cushioned nether regions.

'Ooooh my goodness! it's here, it's here', the scream was one of sheer delight. I honestly cannot tell you how I reached that revelation, but it was there as clear as day, I just knew, and every fibre of my being tingled with excitement as I ran to the house with my news.

Several days passed by before Leigh and David followed up, they had brought in a specialised landscaper and a stonemason to carefully dismantle the raised flower bed in search of the well. Sure enough under mounds of earth and rock was the base row of stone forming what remained of the circular wall around the well, across the well was a large solid iron cover. Earth and ornamental large stones had ensured that routine garden maintenance would not give up the wells secret location.

David and Leigh had been so excited to know where the well was that they invited me to look around their house which had that much residual energy it was like a party. No threatening energy, more like busy and homely but sensing a past tragedy it was good to have free rein to scope the energy properly. Drawn upstairs there was a bedroom to the right, the feelings were that it was a room for storing sacks of grain originally, regardless of the bunk beds in there with typical boy adventure print duvet sets. On the left a door opened up to another bedroom but it felt like a corridor for spirit to pass through and not a restful bedroom. There were two optional routes to the room beyond that, one was to go back downstairs then ascending again by the main stairs or to stay and clamber over a low supporting beam, the beam exit was the chosen option. Clambering over the beam it immediately felt like entering a different dimension.

There was a family bathroom on the left, a master bedroom complete with en suite bathroom at the end of the corridor, a window was effectively positioned on the right. A great feeling of sadness enveloped me as I looked at the window, shocked to see a young man hanging from a pole jutting out above it. I heard an old-fashioned pulley, the air felt dusty it was real but unreal and the glass was no longer there.

Unsettled I went downstairs, Leigh and David eager to hear what had been found led me to their huge open plan living area.' Why can I see people looking down on us from the gallery when there isn't one? 'Easy' said David, 'this is the older part of the building and there was a gallery around the upper level until it was replaced to accommodate the new floor'. Closing my eyes visions of sacks being hauled up on a pulley came to mind, yet the window was a normal window without any signs of agricultural or farm activity but in my mind's eye there was the boy again, was I seeing a picture of how things were so many years previously? The couple were keen to fill me in on the history of the house, how it had been extended several times, the front part had been a barn, a pulley system had hoisted sacks of grain to the upper more dry area for storage. It was there that a farm hand had been found hanging, caught up accidentally while trying to untangle the pulley. Briefly touching on the squealing, chopping noises and smells that had encumbered me with nausea on arrival, it seemed that David and Leigh were not so oblivious after all to the reason. Possibly seeing if I was genuine they had skipped over the initial impact their home had on me but were happy to explain. At one time the outbuilding had been a very busy abattoir, gruesome! An interesting few hours that's for sure, fantastic that the well appeared, but funny too because *I am Me, no one Special*

CHAPTER FIFTEEN

With The Heaviest Of Hearts

Jason and the twins brought so much joy to Mum and Dad as did all their scrumptious grandchildren, when they moved to Cornwall all of us were intent on bringing as much laughter into their life as possible.

Peter and I stood at the top of the steep slope leading down to Fiscal beach, each holding a handle of Dads wheelchair. We said 'Dad! you know when you used to tell us off or stop our pocket money? Revenge is sweet, bye Daddy, he laughed out loud and it was good to hear, as the saying goes 'laughter is the best medicine'. Again, when we pretended to abandon him on the beach as the tide was coming in, waving goodbye to him as we walked off. Sharon and Sheila tormented him but lovingly and his fabulous sense of humour never waned, somewhat warped often sarcastic but always witty never dull and we were without doubt chips off the old block. Back home shortly after a visit I was in the kitchen when a clear vision of Dad played out in front of me, he was being placed into an ambulance and the normally reassuring spirit voices told me that my precious Dad was taking his last journey in this life. Frantically trying to call Mum and Sharon in Cornwall without success confirmed in my mind that all was not good. I phoned the twins father and pleaded with him to come home, he didn't hesitate for one moment knowing and trusting my intuition.

After the quickest explanation, his car was loaded with everything needed when taking toddlers on a road trip, Jason stayed with friends because of school. We headed straight for the local hospital not far from Mum and Dads home in Cornwall, my vision had shown an ambulance, so logic told me that Dad would be there. I ran inside, heart beating like crazy, Sharon fell into my arms and held on tightly breaking into gut wrenching sobs, Dad had just passed as we arrived. Mum had been given the mandatory cup of tea for shock while we kissed our dear Daddy, so sad for his pain and suffering, grateful that his soul was free. He was met by a Naval officer who may have been his father I don't know, and his mother, our dear Grandma Mercie. It is reassuring to know that when we begin our journey to our new address we don't travel alone because our loved ones come for us.

Loss of a parent hits hard because they are supposed to be here for ever, they mould us with their unconditional love into the people we become, they care for us and love us unconditionally yet what do we do for them good enough to repay all they have done? Our hearts were heavy and the sadness for Mum almost unbearable. Strangely I have never seen or felt my father spiritually even though I miss him terribly (and have his nose), but I was told by spirit that he watches over my baby sister Sheila, they had an adorable bond, for that I am happy.

Shortly after Dads passing Mum phoned to say that she had an appointment at another hospital the next day, she told us that she had been having difficulty eating and was rapidly losing weight, worried about her we had been phoning every day making sure that GP appointments went well. Being the stoic person, she was her 'Matron' side took over, never complaining, never giving the complete picture but it was all written down in her little pocket diary, her letters to all of us full of optimistic humour.

The sick niggling feeling would not go away and visions of Mums stomach and abdominal area as a black mass haunted my daily thoughts, I was glad that she had a hospital appointment.

Strange how our instincts and so called second sight works, a few weeks previously I had felt the need to recapture treasured memories, one such memory was of when we came back to England from Singapore.

My parents were invited to a grand RAF ball in Blackpool, so they had booked us into a lovely hotel on the sea front. Sharon and I shared a room overlooking the sea and the vanity basin had Imperial Leather soap in the dish, I kept smelling it, we held hands and danced around that room gloriously happy. To this day the smell of Imperial Leather soap or talc invokes those memories.

In the morning we were gently woken by kind hotel staff saying that Mum and Dad had been injured in an accident coming back from the ball. Dad was seriously injured, Mum had a fractured arm and would be back with us once it had been set. It was a private hotel and so we could live there for a few months and go to St Cuthbert's School (the least said about our school experience the better), we loved the hotel. In those days Blackpool was a thriving seaside town and wonderful place. Peppermint rock, Candy floss and toffee apples, the best ever fish and chips, flavoured rock shaped like babies bottles and dummies or a whole cooked breakfast, such fun. Blackpool Tower was amazing, we attended dance classes there, travelling on trams, playing in rock pools in the search for crabs, the pleasure beach, a miniature village and donkey rides on the beach, the fantastic Blackpool illuminations. One of our shared memories is of what was supposed to be a punishment regime. We were polite well-mannered children by all accounts but were terribly spoiled which manifested every so often in dramatic outbursts worthy of an Oscar. Our so-called punishment was to be taken to the local orphanage, each of us having to forfeit a favourite item to give to the orphanage for the children. The idea behind this regular expedition was to teach us values and remind us of how privileged we were, the intent was to shame us leaving us feeling remorseful and appreciative. Mum would take us there on a tram, bonus! we loved travelling by tram and did so to school each day. Then she would be in the office talking to Matron over a cup of tea while we were banished to our punishment of spending time trying to entertain the children. Wow! Some punishment that was, we had the best fun ever with those children they were brilliant, and we used to hurt from laughing, our pockets were full of sweets for all of us to share sneakily from the hotel staff. Of course, we had to do a deep pretend sigh of boredom each time that was our given punishment. Fabulous memories to last a life time in my mental library.

Those days were so happy that I vowed to take my own children there. Unfortunately the booking was for a week starting on the day of Mums hospital visit. From the hotel I phoned her 'they are doing an exploratory op tomorrow, I'm absolutely fine Valderee Valderar, staff are so kind, and the consultant has explained everything to me' she seemed happy with the lovely attention, 'please don't cut your trip short, Sharon is nearby and will keep you posted. We sat on the pier as the op was scheduled and it felt like cold fingers pressing on my neck, yet the day was warm. My mother needed me, she was dying, the voices in my head urged me to go to her. When we phoned the hospital the staff nurse had been about to phone me asking that we get there as soon as possible. Knowing how far we would be travelling she urged us to drive safely, I had prayed to our angels and knew we would be safe. Her body had been closed almost as soon as it was opened, the black mass of my vision had been cancer and Mum was riddled with it, she was terminally ill. Our beautiful mother was put on palliative care, she suffered so much, in an unprecedented move the staff allowed me to do her nursing care and two students could be mentored by me. Obviously, the drugs round was totally their nursing responsibility for obvious reasons, the students and I spoke of dignity and respect something high on Mums list in her Matron role. My partner became a hero as he attended to our twins needs, taking all the worry from me. I will never forget the support he gave to me during those times.

We loved and tended to our 'patient', it was cathartic being proactive in Mums care, as the cancer stole some of the dignity she so valued Mum would have been mortified. Knowing that hearing is the last sense to go we talked as we brushed her hair, moisturised her heels and kept her hydrated, she would try to smile or squeeze our hands in response. Peter had been to see Mum and my sisters had done lots of lovely things, so it was my turn now to be strong and seeing Mums face distorted with pain was heart breaking.

As I was praying hard for the angels to release her from pain because her soul was truly beautiful the Cornish sister in charge of Mum's care put her hand on my arm affectionately. 'Go and have your shower Valerie, we will look after Mummy for you' she hugged me as I stood up and I knew that those prayers were about to be answered, Returning, I noticed an aura of gentle peace around my mother, walking to the nurses station I looked at the staff and said 'thank you from the bottom of my heart', each one had tears falling down their cheeks. They realised that I knew more than what any of us could word and that I was truly grateful for their loving compassion. Minutes later my partner arrived, and night staff baby sat for us, Mum had been moved to a side room, her face no longer contorted by unbearable pain looked peaceful. Suddenly Mummy opened her beautiful turquoise blue eyes and stared upwards, holding out her arms she was smiling 'Peter' she cried, Aunty Mima, Jean, Barbara, Aunty Cicely, Daddy You're all here, yes I'm ready'. With that she closed her eyes and her soul began its journey. One keepsake memory is of Mums smile as she passed and the certainty that my father (Peter senior), Mums Dad, her aunties and my two sisters had come to take her with them, feeling sure that Grandma Jane Eleanor would be waiting for her. We were blessed to see such a gentle passing for Mummy surrounded with love, we will never dismiss her suffering, Mums face contorted with pain is a memory I keep. But the strength I have from seeing her smile of recognition as her family in spirit took her to what is now classed as Higher Life will always inspire me. My partner was unable to see spirit but he was fully aware of something very special happening. We both said that had we just seen Mum suffering so horrifically not looking like herself, we would have been traumatised, but we witnessed her total peace and the changes that brought my beautiful Mummy back to us.

CHAPTER SIXTEEN

When Friends Are The Family You Choose

It is always good to see that our loved ones in spirit have a great sense of humour and when we laugh it is a higher vibration that draws our loved ones close. Sometimes even in the saddest of times I will have a message from someone in spirit that will make me laugh out loud. This is one such story, but first a bit of background for you to know a little about life in the run up to the tragic loss of a very dear friend. Still doing some agency nursing on nights while the children were small I had joined the Ambulance service as you know from the car incident, it was Fred who encouraged me to apply. Because it wasn't all classroom based for our initial training and we were let loose so to speak it was lovely being in the service. We had the best trainers who were fun, with colleagues I adored and would have done anything for. It was just the best job ever in those days, we had time to nurture because there was less pressure.

A huge part of our day while training was ferrying elderly people to and from day hospitals, doing maternity transfers, ex red journeys or white journeys. Ex red are patients taken to A&E as an emergency, treated then not regarded as serious enough for admission. We would take them home and with permission from Control (as it was then) make a cup of tea, light the fire, help them into bed etc, we all loved our job. A white journey would usually be one not classed as a blue light emergency but as an urgent within an hour GP referral. Our ambulance journeys were made as comfortable as possible no matter whose turn it was to drive or attend to the patient, we cherished those in our care. Classroom days were truly rewarding, and the hands-on days were just lovely, have you ever loved your job so much that every day was a new fulfilling adventure? that is how I was. I learned about patient handling not just medical skills but most of all I found true, deep, loving friendships. Those that last forever, that are unselfish, warm and thoughtful, those that care and protect, those that equally share the work load and those that make a cup of coffee to welcome you back on station. Ian my partner in crime was just adorable we were always laughing and our vehicle shone, we took such pride in it. We shared stories and secrets so when he decided that blood and guts were not for him I was distraught. Our friendship though is forever, and I love him dearly, he is a truly special person and lights up my life. Following Ian's change of career Fred was partnered with me more often, he had a friend named Steve they were inseparable, the three of us became 'besties'. Like the three Musketeers all for one and one for all, they were loving uncles to my children and I couldn't imagine life without them in it. So close were we that when I was offered a job at Stansted Airport with an Air Ambulance Repatriation company, the boys moved to the airport too. Our Ambulance Service family was happy for us knowing that our new work would overlap into theirs still.

Life was hectic but fun, never knowing where I would be flying with seriously ill patients from day to day. I also ran a dream team of young adults who were part of an Air Line initiative to give passengers a worry-free journey. Anyone vulnerable would be taken through the system by a team member, all their needs cared for whether in a wheelchair, unwell or pregnant. As a company we mostly collected or returned people overseas or in the UK too ill to travel without medical assistance. Our boss who was an ex-Army Captain flew the helicopter but when need arose chartered small fixed wing aircraft or booked blocks of seats that were configurated for stretchers on long haul commercial flights. The work I did was demanding because I also had to check out medical facilities in airports across Europe for the Air Line and for potential air ambulance patients. Should ever need arise to replace IV fluids, do dressings or re assess prior to continuing on to receiving hospitals etc. all would be smooth, Steve and Fred were often instrumental in the success of a good flight for various reasons, exhausting times but laughter made the long hours whizz by. My fantastic little gang will always have a huge piece of my heart.

I was a single mum again by this time and the twins had been adopted by some of the staff who would make up beds for them in crew rooms, take them for fabulous evenings or days out and meals in the Under-croft staff canteen. They had visitor passes in those days when every other person wasn't a potential terror threat, they met flight crews and airport staff who spoiled them rotten, they went with us to celebrity football matches when I covered as a medic for them in between rugby medical duties. Juggling life was a challenge but being surrounded by love every day we thrived happily, all three children loved it when our house was full of those very people who showed that whatever happened would be in our corner. Steve mostly worked in cargo, so we saw him often, then one day Fred phoned to say that Steve had joined some old pals on a trip overseas for work. He had sort of mentioned it previously with his initial reason being to help his very sick brother financially. Sadly, his dear brother passed before that could happen and when we were with Steve at the funeral we just assumed that he wouldn't go and were relieved. However, after being offered shed loads of money Steve leapt at the chance, he was to our horror going to fight as a Mercenary (a hired soldier).

For months no contact or news from our absent musketeer we were worried, things settled somewhat, life continued, Steve's choice was reluctantly accepted with heavy hearts. The day that things changed will never be erased mentally. After an obscenely early start at work I arrived home and was going upstairs to change, a voice was coming from the bedroom and I realised that someone was leaving a telephone message. Steve's voice was saying ' and you are the best friend anyone could ever have, love you babe for ever' Running to pick up before the phone went dead I lunged at the receiver shouting ' Steve I'm here don't hang up' his breathing was low but audible I felt his immense sadness, he stayed silent so those were the last words I would ever hear our darling friend say. 'Steve, Steve what has happened, where are you? I'm coming to get you and look after you sweetheart, where are you? I love you' my words echoed in the phone as it went dead. Ice cold fear swept over my body as I replayed Steve's poignant message, thanking me for being in his life, for loving him unconditionally, I was sure that this was Steve's goodbye and that he was about to take his own life. I phoned the police in his county, police who knew me from the airport in a medical capacity. 'Hello, I am so sorry to trouble you, this is Valerie the Mad Medic from Stansted Airport urgently requesting assistance '. They could not have been nicer and immediately asked how they could help, 'without any doubt my friend Steve is going to take his own life'. As I gave Steve's address I could picture clearly where he was, he wasn't at home I relayed that to the police, the officer knew that I was serious and bless him so much he trusted my intuition. 'There is a country road branching at some point to a very narrow lane with really high embankments, the field at the end of it is mushy and I visualise old aircraft there at one time and can see a rickety Hangar, he is in a small red car'. Straight away the officer called for back-up, he was sure of the location and would contact me as soon as he had news. Never having been to Steve's house because he moved prior to going overseas I didn't know where it was or the surrounding area, but in my head, it was as clear as Google search is now. An hour later the same officer spoke to me, it was to confirm what I had suspected, he apologised profusely for being unable to save the dear man Fred and I were proud to call our friend. The police were kind and wanted to know what they could do to help me; their empathy was massively appreciated. 'Just a couple of things please', I said, 'had he shaved his cheeky moustache off as I can't see it and he swore never to shave it? – answer 'yes', was he wearing a Ban the Bomb pendant? I can see one –answer 'yes', Steve had sent a vision of himself to my memory as he had passed. Last time Fred and I saw him he was wearing his little trademark tash and sported a St. Christopher.

Steve had been found in a small red car on an old airfield as I visualised, a Hangar in the distance. Fred said that while Steve had been fighting overseas his team had rescued a little girl wounded in warfare and orphaned. Evidently he tried every avenue to get the girl into the UK for safety but oodles of red tape prevented it, Steve could not eat or sleep knowing the little girls inevitable fate. The pain was too much for him to bear, in his eyes he was a failure, subsequently he took his own life. The police officer had accepted my insight without question. I thanked him from the bottom of my heart for his compassion, he gave his contact number for Fred and I to talk to him if we needed to, then said 'that is quite a skill you have'.

But I Am Only Me, No One Special

For days I cried and cried for the loss of such a precious friend until each rib hurt, even with the knowledge that he would have healing and be loved, in spirit he would achieve peace.

One day I cried so much that my eyes puffed up, so not an attractive look and blow me I heard Cheeky Steve's voice randomly out of the blue. Loud and clear it went 'Val, (he and Fred were the only people who got away with calling me Val, because I'm Valerie) stop crying babe, your eyes are like two piss holes in the snow', I laughed and laughed then phoned his wife who also laughed, reassured by that and we both knew somehow that Steve was alright. Steve had a fantastic somewhat warped sense of humour and how comforting that he still has it regardless of how rude. As I said before, laughter does draw spirit to us because of the higher vibrational level. So never feel guilty for the days you manage to laugh following bereavement, it isn't inappropriate our loved ones want to hear our laughter.

CHAPTER SEVENTEEN

Lynette

Paul, my partner came into the life of our family just over twenty years ago and because my colleagues were mostly men he wasn't sure how our relationship would be. He has from day one cherished me but for a while he was prone to quite dark moods occasionally, whenever he was unsure. Our dear friend Lynette a gifted Trance Medium was also my mentor, teaching me a great deal about spirit, how to channel and protect myself etc, she was famous but fabulously down to earth, completely without ego or false promises. Lynette and I hatched a devious plot to help Paul and it was arranged that together with Lynette's wonderful husband Tony we would have dinner at their lovely home. Lord and Lady Dagenham as we call them made us truly welcome and dinner was really delicious. Afterwards Lynette winked at me and said 'okay my darling, let's do some meditation together it will help with your spiritual progression', I replied 'that will be good thank you, just what I need'. Paul was invited to join us so somewhat nervously and a tadge bored seated himself comfortably as he followed our lead, eyes closed, hands relaxed open on laps, three deep breaths slowly in through the nose exhaled slowly through the mouth, Lynette spoke the instructions in a low soothing tone.

Because it was for Pauls benefit my brain hadn't switched to meditation mode or so I thought, nevertheless I went with the flow and followed routinely. This is weird, what's happening? I felt myself growing taller, with hands that felt larger and masculine, Palms upwards, arms stretched in front of me, eyes still closed I saw a Faberge type egg about 24 inches tall beautifully hand carved. It was resting in my hands, it opened, and I saw Jesus wearing a crown of thorns with blood trickling down his face, with arms outstretched he looked into my eyes and said, 'suffer little children to come unto me', then my hands were empty.

A huge eye appeared very much like the eye on the well-known television show 'Big Brother' but with vivid hues of turquoise and purple.

In the far distance Lynette's voice broke into my meditative state, it felt like coming around from anaesthetic, my eyes wanted to stay closed. 'Something happened to you darling' said Lynette not surprised in any way, 'do you want to talk about it?', Paul looked on warily, all of this so new to him. Lynette was ecstatic as she made sense of what had occurred, I had recounted the feelings and visualisations that had been given to me so clearly during a strange but fascinating experience. It had been totally unexpected, our intention had been to encourage Paul to relax and put his days of the dark moods away for good. Lynette said that for some reason I had regressed and evidently lived life as a man totally at home on the land, I looked like an Indian scout wearing just a loin cloth and there were three horses without saddles near to me, another horse had slipped into the river which had burst its banks. Lynette said that I was very masculine and strong. 'You fell into the river trying to rescue your horse, the river was lapping across the land and you were surrounded by rushing, brown coloured water, it was too fast, and you went under fighting for breath before you passed. It all made so much sense, my inherent fear of dirty water, floods, Mucky beck etc. I knew then that somehow it would have to be dealt with and it was.

Carrying on, Lynette said 'Valerie how beautiful! seeing our Lord in your vision, do you realise how blessed you are? you are being acknowledged by spirit for your work with children and they are telling you that it is right for you. The huge eye represents your third eye and how you are developing your psychic awareness'. It was all very emotional, Lynette and I were in tears, I was grateful but humbled by such an amazing experience, after all *I Am Me, No One Special*. We both looked across at Paul expecting him to be overwhelmed as he regaled his own exciting episode, after all this was supposed to be wonderful and healing for him. 'How was that for you darling? Said Lynette, 'what did it do for you?' I added, waiting with happy anticipation only to have 'bugger all!' as his deflated response. Disappointed but understanding of how the universe and world of spirit have their reasons, all we could do was laugh. Paul wasn't the least bit worried, he took it all in his stride and soon managed to put the days of dark moods way behind him. Such is the grand tapestry of life.

CHAPTER EIGHTEEN

Spiritual Mayhem at tea time

The expression, these things are sent to try us is ensconced in my brain because challenges in life are part and parcel of most people's daily life, our family is no exception. My personal daily schedule is annoying at times but rewarding at others so there probably is some sort of balance.

The nursing agency asked if I could cover a triple shift from Sunday lunch time until Monday morning at 08-00, the shift was far too long for most people. For Data protection I will refer to the patient as Nelly.

Arriving at the house I noted that it was large but homely looking, the girl on duty did the briefest of hand overs muttering that she couldn't wait to get home, before practically catapulting herself through the door. Our patient was really demanding yet was not in any obvious pain or discomfort, neither hungry or thirsty, she appeared to revel in calling back whoever was on duty the minute they left. It didn't take Freud to calculate a severe case of loneliness and that the pattern of her demands pushed people away instead of engaging them positively. Having convinced her using lots of medical jargon that it could make her poorly using the commode up to 55 times a day (reflected in her notes), I asked her what would make her happy. There began a lovely rapport between us and many months of Sunday triple shifts. Nelly's family would visit most Sunday afternoons, so I started taking baking ingredients and spare equipment in to leave there. Prior to family visits I would put ingredients into bowls on a large tray and Nelly in bed would add them to the mixing bowl. Nelly loved this and would proudly offer 'her baking' to family, she would be shown the cakes mid baking so that she could advise me how much longer they needed, that way she was still in control of her home, vitally important.

Nelly's son Geoff soon got wise to the little tactics employed to bring a bit of oomph back and he even built a special cupboard for the baking things. It was great, very well designed with the inside slightly sloping back to prevent items falling out, it had an old fashioned ball socket opening that needed a firm tug to access the contents, this is relevant to my story so please bear with me. The cupboard was above a work top, so it was geared for health and safety.

One Sunday afternoon the family turned up and we wheeled Nelly through into the big bay windowed lounge from her bedroom (dining room conversion with lovely French windows). Tea and cake duly served by me in 'earth mother' role, I went upstairs to the spacious front bedroom that also boasted a huge bay window. My study books were in there for later when Nelly would be sleeping, I would then sit in the lounge to be near to her room.

The housekeeper was due to get married and under masses of pressure, way behind with incidentals like invitations and favours etc. I wanted to help. Out came the ironing board from the laundry room, I resolved to clear some of her tasks to free her for wedding tasks. Ironing away, it was soothing seeing the cricketers wearing their dapper whites very British, watching families enjoying picnics as they watched. CRAAASH! BANG! CLATTER! The noises echoed upstairs from the kitchen, I ran downstairs in time to see the puzzled family gathered by the kitchen door.

The new cupboard was wide open, its contents strewn across the floor how could that be? Flour, tins, currants, bun cases and glace cherries etc everywhere. As we gazed in shocked surprise the washing machine went into a bumpy spin jigging about as clothes tossed and turned in the drum. Nothing strange there you may think but as Geoff reached over to turn it off the machine wasn't even plugged in.

Assuring the family that I was fine with it and would soon clear the mess up they said a lightning goodbye to Nelly, thanked me profusely and practically ran to their car. Once Nelly was settled into bed around 9-00 pm off I trotted upstairs to get my study books, the landing light popped and went off, a regular occurrence inconvenient at times but no big deal. Electricians had checked and rechecked insisting that all was well, and no faults could be found, we just accepted it. Grabbing my deluxe kidskin briefcase, sorry! I fibbed then, grabbing my Tesco carrier bags I turned to go downstairs and heard loud knocking on the door, nothing strange there you may say. But when that door is not the front door, is invisible and less than a foot away it is pretty frightening, I ran like the wind, major Adrenaline rush. Thankfully the night was incident free and during handover I asked the two staff if they had ever heard spooky knocking, thought it better not to mention the kitchen incident. 'Why do you think that everyone is leaving? ' they said, one of the girls told me that she was so fed up with changing lightbulbs that she stood on the landing and shouted 'if you think you are that clever push me down the stairs I dare you', that particular girl does Reiki and works with crystals so her behaviour was really against the grain. She started walking down the stairs watched by her colleague at the foot of the stairs who had been curious about what had sparked such a cross response. Her curiosity had turned to a scream as 'confrontational girl' was propelled at speed slamming on to the floor winded and shocked. 'I was pushed! **It** pushed me, OMG I was pushed' confrontational girl had then screamed to her friend. Both girls were now on their last shift at Nelly's far too afraid to return.

When telling Paul later that day, he was concerned for me especially when I made the decision not to confront the lively spirit but to address it on my next shift there.

On the following weekend Nelly was sleeping soundly after her lunch so again I went upstairs to find something to do that would take pressure off the housekeeper. Firstly, though I had a very important task to carry out. Taking a deep breath and going through all of the small rituals carried out when asking for Holy protection I addressed whoever was visiting from spirit. Would it make a difference because after all *I Am Me, No One Special*?

Strangely enough, despite the antics and startling noises whatever entity was in the house never felt threatening or evil so my feelings were more apprehensive than afraid. Even after my colleague was pushed, it felt that she had upset something desperate to have our attention, she had abused spiritual boundaries, she was startled but unhurt and very contrite. Boldly I stood in the centre of the large front bedroom and said 'hello my spirit friends, please may I ask if we are doing something that you are unhappy with, because if we are I really am so sorry, - nothing no response. Continuing 'please let me know how we can make things better because to be honest the knocking noises, cupboards emptying and lightbulbs popping, not to mention the poor girl shoved on the stairs are frightening.

'My name is Joseph' said a gentle masculine voice, *'I am Nelly's husband, when she was pregnant I wrote a book about our life, it was during the war'.* Carrying on *'Nell was always a demanding woman and would never go into the air raid shelter, so I carried her. I built the shelter myself at the top of the garden near to the fields'.*

Josephs parting words were *'The book is in a biscuit tin on Nell's trolley by her bed, by the way lassie that tall girl looks through all of the drawers and tells people personal things, we don't like it'.*

Thanking Joseph for coming through to me I made a 'memo to self' to check out the top of the garden and to carry out safeguarding procedures to protect Nelly from the type of abuse inflicted by the tall nurse, zero tolerance. No sooner had Joseph gone, a soothingly beautiful voice came in, it was the voice of a young woman and she said *'I'm Susan, Nelly and Josephs daughter, I had to leave my beautiful children behind I passed too soon from breast cancer, please talk to the nosey nurse'.*

Wow I'm on a roll here I thought after I had thanked Susan for trusting me. This is better than I ever imagined and hopefully it is time to sort things to allow Nelly's loved ones to rest peacefully. Before I had chance to do anything a refined soft voice held my attention, *'hello dear I'm Mrs. Jones from next door, I lived there for many years and was happy when Nelly's dear brother bought the house when I passed. Do you know dear? that nurse takes things too and she sleeps in Susan's room at night instead of looking after Nelly'*. 'Oh Mrs. Jones, thank you so much for telling me, I am really sad that these things have been happening and am going to sort it, is this why we have been hearing the knocks etc.?' I asked tentatively. *'Yes, dear I'm afraid it is'*. With that Mrs. Jones disappeared and all was quiet, not knowing if they could still hear me and feeling a bit shell shocked at the clarity of the spiritual messages I spoke anyway. 'Thank you for sharing with me, that means a lot, I promise to sort things out and whenever I come here will always say hello to you'. There was a peaceful silence in the room, had that all been a figment of my imagination, it was surreal that's for sure.

Once Nelly was wide awake and had eaten breakfast I asked her about the war and how it was living there during that time, she laughed and told me about her husband carrying her with her baby bump up to the air raid shelter. As an afterthought she pointed to a pile of folded scarves on her bedside trolley and told me to look underneath them, there was an old biscuit tin with the Queen's coronation picture on it, I was told to open it. There indeed was the book written by Joseph all those years ago, I was elated and wanted to yell with excitement, how amazing, poor Nelly almost suffocated from the hugs that were impossible to hold back. I loved the book Joseph. Colleagues arrived for handover, little knowing then that very soon the spiritual activity would end, I had someone to report first.

Walking to the top of the extensive grounds sure enough a door nestled amongst the shrubbery it was the entrance to Joseph's air raid shelter, what a truly privileged experience, one always valued.

Confronting the tall nurse, she boasted that she knew how much money was in Nelly's bank account and how much the housekeeper was paid, no shame or guilt just a smug cocky expression. I was beyond livid so being professional and following protocol was very difficult, my disgust knew no bounds. It is a privilege to be in someone's home not a right, we were trusted and she abused that trust, she didn't even flinch when she was informed that my duty of care required me to report her. It was no longer a rumour that she pried, but it was my secret as to how I knew.

I always remembered to say hello at the start of each shift, the negative activity ceased, the family confirmed their loved one's identity and had great comfort knowing that they are around.

CHAPTER NINETEEN

Random 'Stuff'

Random experiences littered my life so much that there was never time to feel lonely or bored, on one such occasion I popped into the post office in a nearby village, queueing behind an elderly lady. Sadness emanated from every single pore and her heart ached with loss, beside her stood her loving husband reaching for her hand in a gesture of comfort. It was a gesture that went unnoticed in her sorrowful grief, her dead husband had passed to higher life and she could no longer feel the loving touch of his warm hand. As the lady left I approached her with trepidation and introduced myself, fearing at first that she would judge me as a menopausal crackpot and bash me over the head with the yummy looking French stick in her bag I was cautious. Pale blue eyes looked me over, she walked as though her joints ached with every ailment age loads us up with, her soft smile gave a glimpse into the beauty that was once hers to enjoy.

Please forgive the intrusion, I know that you trust in spirit and that your husband has just passed, she wasn't fazed at all and wanted to know more.

Hearing that her much loved husband was by her side and that I was able to validate his presence by the things he had asked me to tell her brought so much joy. The look of happiness was priceless, I thanked them both for letting me be part of that.

Loving children the way I do it is always emotional when I see them spiritually but knowing how cherished and loved they are is comforting. Seeing a young mother curled up on her sofa or chair feet tucked up cosily, not always for comfort but for the loss she feels every day is sad. On days when the pain is slightly easier to bear she would probably freak out if she knew why. Snuggled up in the contours of her body is the much longed for baby who touched the earth and was gone in the blink of an eye, back to bring comfort to mum. Our loved ones in spirit let their presence be known in many ways, it is being astute or trusting enough that enables us to be aware of it.

Have you ever been sleeping but sense pressure on the bed, enough to wake you up and question what you felt? It can happen any time but more often it does so in the early hours, Most times it will feel like a cat kneading the covers with its little paws (affectionately known as 'baking bread'). Usually its subtle enough to make us believe that it is pure imagination but trust me, unless you suffer with restless leg syndrome or have twitchy limbs, you more than likely have a loved one spending time with you. By the way, our loved ones include beloved pets usually cats and dogs but others too although I wouldn't really want to feel a horse trampling on my bed.

Lynette once told me that while doing a spiritual church service followed by clairvoyance, she received a lovely message, it had the congregation laughing out loud. My friend had been facing her audience from the podium and even she was surprised at the message that came through for one of the eager people seated near the front. 'I have a dog and a frog walking towards me down the aisle' she said, 'can anyone take that? The audience giggled, my friend giggled, it turned to laughter and laughter being infectious soon had everyone joining in. A dear lady raised her hand timidly 'I can take that, all eyes were on her as she spoke. 'I had a dog that I loved dearly, he was in a way my child and he spent his summers beside our goldfish pond as I sat nearby knitting. The warmer the day the longer he would be out there, we noticed that Storm had a tiny companion, a frog would jump up onto his back and sit there all day, it would move a little so that Storm could lick it almost as though he was being groomed by the frog'. The lady dabbed her eyes and continued, it was lovely to see, and the little frog never seemed to mind when my husband and I had afternoon tea beside them. When Storm died months later we no longer saw the frog, we grieved for both of them and couldn't face sitting near the pond'.

Lynette thanked the lady for sharing such a wonderful story of friendship, 'they both thank you for loving them and wanted you to know that not only were they connected on earth but are connected in spirit. They will always be on the same soul path and ask you not to be sad'. I just love the energy that emanates whenever my friend graces her platform sessions, far from being sad for those newly bereaved, her sessions bring comfort, love and joy to almost everyone in her audience. Because *I Am Me, No One Special* my spiritual stuff is by the by and still surprises me, yet at the same time I truly value what a huge privilege it is to be a tiny part of such an incredible realm. I stand in awe of people who have developed their mediumship where they give comfort to many, bringing love and light in vast amounts as they beautifully connect with spirit. Being, in the presence of gifted spiritual mediums is very humbling especially dear Tony Stockwell who brings love and laughter in bucket loads. Dear Lynette is like the female version of Tony, she is funny, kind and caring, both are approachable and warm. They provide the true essence of spiritual honour and fabulous energy for connecting with spirit, we have some much loved local Mediums who bring a lot of comfort, I am not going to mention them in case I miss anyone special out, but I see how devoted to helping people they are. It was during one of Lynette's evening sessions that I was approached by an elderly lady who walked up to me looking intently, 'you have Mother Teresa behind you, in front of you and either side of you' she said before hugging me and grabbing a cup of tea from the counter, all very matter of fact. Tears sprang to my eyes I was feeling massively unworthy of the association, wondering what was happening to warrant such a highly esteemed visitor. The ladies statement left me quite emotional because with today's climate of terror and violence we are almost forced to dwell on bad people and awful events. It is all far too easy to forget how many amazing people there are in the world, those who are awe inspiring, dedicated souls carrying out the most amazing work yet graced with humility because they cannot see their own wonder.

So! Why on earth me? My life's purpose is a teeny drop of help in an endless ocean of need, others do far greater things, I was meant to do my little effort for humanity therefore it doesn't count. It may not be much, but I am passionate about protecting children, well not just children, anyone vulnerable needing someone in their corner.

CHAPTER TWENTY

Walerie (Valerie) Mummy

Good grief, can you believe that in January I completed my 20th year of caring for Street and Railway Children in Mumbai and have started my 21st year. Multi visits initially each year until it became too expensive, in later years the trips have dwindled to once a year for many reasons, one is of course the enormous cost another is the time and effort each trip takes to plan and organise amid endless commitments. Not many people realise that I am in contact every day with Mumbai, checking on my children and having updates to make sure that they are safe. They need survival items that friends drop off for me on stop over flights on route to other destinations. A child may need surgery out of the blue, there might be a crisis I need contacts in Mumbai to sort for me. Each trip and project are almost a year in planning, so my aim is to work on a project each year to ensure a useful positive impact. There are hundreds of children under the umbrella of my care clinically and therapeutically, they attend my pop-up street clinics, or I visit the vast slum areas. Since the horrific 2007 Mumbai Terror attacks we have been doing craft workshops following each medical session, they are therapeutic. The bonus being that the children sell what they make, they are learning fun skills in a safe environment, earning honest money and not taking the risks associated with begging or stealing. It does wonders for their self-esteem too. Of course, it isn't black and white because many children are forced into begging to keep a family member in drugs or cheap alcohol. So, anything they make is stolen from them and sometimes destroyed in a selfish act of belittling a child more skilled than themselves.

Grandma Jane Eleanor's presence is like a shield as she walks alongside me, there are times when my life has been in danger even having a gun pressed at my forehead on one rescue, but I felt her presence and drew strength from it.

Because this life journey was planned out for me in the huge Universal book it feels like the most normal thing to do and it makes me proud to be Walerie Mummy (no one can say Valerie). With my angels and Grandma guiding me, their love and protection is like a beautiful Talisman. I love and honour the children to whom my life is so easily dedicated to heart and soul as Mummy.

In Hinduism Angels are not recognised as such but they have deities called 'Devas' (or shining ones), Devas are also recognised in Buddhism. In both Hinduism and Buddhism Devas act in similar angelic ways to the angel's that we love. People who believe in Devas (male)and Devi's (female) say that they are assigned especially to guard people, animals and plants helping them to prosper and grow. The reason they are called 'shining ones' is because they have achieved spiritual enlightenment, they act like divine energy. They are equivalent and powerful.

Since being told that Blessed Mother Teresa is with me, those exact words have been given to me twice more by two different Mediums in two different places, the emotion I felt each time was weepy and humble. Why would our beloved Mother of Kolkata spend time with me a scatty disorganised blonde lady from Essex, it was too much to take in and was overwhelming. It took a long time to accept, but three different Mediums in three different places saying the same thing word for word was incredible, they were unaware of what I do in India with the Street and Railway Children, *SPOOKY!* to say the least. But having wondered why for ages, I have reconciled to the fact that Mother Teresa is not trying to give me ideas above my station or a reason to show off, she is in fact my supervisor, I can handle that. What fortune! how lucky am I? one thing is for sure, my promise to always love, cherish and protect the children became even more determined. It is strange how life rolls on and

how much is connected quite fascinatingly we just
need to take time and trust our instinctive feelings
to recognise the signs helping our journey along.

CHAPTER TWENTY-ONE

What A Small World

One place in Mumbai that I used to visit each year when the Mother Superior and many of the Sisters who were friends of mine there is St Elizabeth's Hospital in Malabar Hill Mumbai. I spent time with the Sisters and patients, going into intensive care, neo-natal intensive care, theatre and the wards for several hours at a time. The Sister's used to introduce me as Walerie who sees people we would share tea and biscuits with them in their quarters, chatting about many different things, never boring.

Early on I discovered that several of the Sisters there used to spend a year in the UK at St. Elizabeth's in Much Hadham, Essex, what a small world. I have some friends all connected to the hospital here. Carolyn still works there with the residents and students in a huge way, her mother Joan used to work in the offices and Barbara was a Mother Superior with a great love for the pastoral side of things. All three have been involved in the many events at St. Elizabeth's. Barbara had Parkinson's disease which gradually became debilitating, so Joan became her *carer* with Carolyn fully involved too. One day in the run up to one of the Mumbai trips I asked the ladies if they would like me to deliver post by hand to their friends at the Mumbai St. Elizabeth's. Barbara asked if it was possible to post some mail from my base to another address in Mumbai adding that she thought it too far away to deliver by hand, no problem at all it would be a pleasure. Taking the mail from Barbara I didn't even glance at the address and it was packed safely in my case that afternoon. As soon as I unpacked in Mumbai one of my priorities was to buy stamps for Barbara's mail, talk about 'gob smacked' looking at the address I laughed in disbelief.

It was being sent to a convent directly opposite the shop where I buy supplies for craft workshops. Approximately 40 - 50 minutes away on good traffic days by auto rickshaw from the hotel, what a random coincidence especially as we were scheduled to go there the next day.

It was after lunch when my travelling companions and I delivered said mail we trod carefully aware that the Sisters would be resting. A deliberate decision was made not to ring the bell that would announce our arrival as it was very loud, instead we approached the young novice on reception asking her not to wake the Sisters. Handing the mail over we quietly introduced ourselves, the novice was wide eyed and asked 'are you Walerie who sees people?', we all laughed but she ran to the bell clanging it like crazy shouting 'its Walerie who sees people . The convent had gorgeous old fashioned wooden floors and all we could hear was feet running, several Sisters arrived and with huge affection made us welcome with kind hospitality. It seemed that word had gone around via the Sisters at St. Elizabeth's to various other convents and children's homes and many of them already knew of me a little through my work with children, many names were familiar to me. We enjoyed spending time with the Sisters, hearing about their wonderful work, taking everything in, seeing their humility and passion. I caught a glimpse of something near one of the more mature Sister's, sadness surrounded her, so I asked her who the young man was standing next to her in spirit. Reassuring her that he was very happy and had thanked her for her daily prayers for him, she said that it was her nephew who had passed tragically leaving the whole family devastated. It was good being able to validate his presence with things he said that only she could know and also to give messages for his family. Sister felt that we were meant to be there that day, it was probably a happy coincidence but whatever it was I am grateful for the lovely smile on the Sisters face and the chance visit from her nephew.

India is such a vibrantly spiritual place and very much my second home, it is also where my instincts have often yielded positive spiritual experiences along with the feeling that I have always belonged.

Friends in Mumbai are loving and kind they took me into their hearts from my very first trip, extending that welcome to all of my travel companions over the years and in the process becoming extended family. The children are grown up but still treat me like a queen and would do anything for me, I am positively spoiled with love and attention. Love is energising, it enables me to rescue children and value the wonderful people I am truly blessed to have in my life.

CHAPTER TWENTY-TWO

Angels Rescue The Day

This is where once again Angels have stepped in to help the children.

Prior to one of my first Mumbai trips I had worked every hour possible without dropping yet needed another £ 138-54 to buy a half decent paediatric stethoscope, plus resus bag and mask. Knowing that I would not have any spare money to buy those much-needed pieces of medical kit I asked my angels for help. First, the reason I asked is because we have free will and they don't interfere with that, I usually say why we need something before I ask. I thanked them for listening to me about the reason the money was needed adding that I didn't mind having to work extra hard, then again thanked them lovingly. Adding, In Love and Light, In Love and Light, In Love and Light, (the power of three) like the Holy Trinity. Within minutes the phone rang, it was an insurance company, 'Hi Valerie, please can you help us tonight, we are flying a patient to Liverpool from London and you are the perfect person for this flight'. Slight pause! 'oh, we will get you back in time for work tomorrow, you can snack at the receiving hospital then eat properly on the flight back'. The co-ordinator added 'you can doze on the way to London and on the way back from London as a driver will ferry you to City Airport and back, please please say yes'. I would have said yes after the first please in gratitude for them choosing me. The Medical transfer just flowed, our patient was a little sweetie who enjoyed the foot massage I gave her then slept well. Paper work and handover stress free. Back in London the driver collected me and handed over an envelope, not expecting much as it was a short flight, fast handover, no complicated clinical procedures just routine checks and monitoring. Bearing in mind that it was about 19 years ago, I could have spat feathers, inside the envelope was an invoice yes, you've guessed £ 138-54 (quite a lot of money back then even after deductions), if that doesn't knock your socks off I'm not sure what can. The Captain had rounded the money off to £150 he also gave me a bag of lovely soft bandages. I thanked my angels profusely for recognising that my plea was for the higher good.

CHAPTER TWENTY-THREE

The Monday Gang And Bren

Earlier I mentioned Joan, Barbara and Carolyn all of whom I love dearly, Carolyn is married to kind funny Alex, all of us were close friends of Bob and Brenda. Along with other friends we would meet regularly for lunch part of an initiative set up to support people suffering from Parkinson's disease or other debilitating conditions, we would have activities and such plus days out. We noticed that Brenda (Bren) was struggling to do the heavy-duty care that Bob needed, she fractured an ankle so badly that a beautiful Polish girl was allocated ultimately to care for Bob but also to assist Bren. I will name this lovely young lady Bella, they loved her like a daughter and their dog who could be quite antisocial at home adored her she just belonged in their life. Nothing was too much trouble for Bella, Bob and Bren thrived, spending many happy times with her. When Bella for whatever daft reason was sent to another live-in post in a different county it was difficult, and Bob was moved into a nearby nursing home. Chosen by Bren, it was a lovely home with excellent care, a move that had to happen for their continued safety. Visiting daily with their dog Susie in tow a routine was established. Shortly afterwards we noticed that Bren kept feeling poorly and was having difficulty keeping food down if she could tolerate it. Bren missed Bob and Bella so we all tried to rally round but were deeply concerned. Basically, our lovely Bren had lots of tests and medical procedures the results of which were devastating, our dear precious friend had pancreatic cancer.

Having tea one day by our pond Bren said 'I know that I'm dying Valerie, that's why I needed to sit with you by your pond', Cuddling her and listening to her it would have been wrong to whisper words of hope and encouragement because she had resigned herself and accepted that she would be called very soon to her higher life, she wouldn't have trusted me. Instead we shared companionable tales and fun memories our friendship forever set in stone, I dreaded losing her and that seems so selfish, when she was the one suffering. An amazingly brave lady Bren struggled through her pain to leave everything in order, it was all catalogued neatly and methodically her wishes lain out immaculately written. But the thing that touched all of us the most was that Bren had interviewed families to adopt Susie dog to ensure that her 'baby' with paws would be happy. A delightful family of Dad, Mum, two boys and a dog with attitude began by visiting Susie at home play dates followed then doggie sleepovers at their house plus walks in the park together. It was their home where prior to Bren passing, Susie settled in, what a truly brave selfless act by Bren. As Bren left this earth I felt certain that a special pair of wings would be waiting for her.

Bella phoned to ask if I'd go with her and a friend (named Roz for now) to see Bren in the chapel of rest. Rushing home after night shift and quickly changing clothes I dashed off to Hertfordshire to the address given. I could park in a nearby centre because I did a day of counselling there each week and I could walk from there to where I hoped the chapel of rest would be. The lumpy bits of pavement were slippery and damp so my concentration was safety focused. Arriving at the address I switched off my two phones and joined the girls in the chapel already with Bren. Both very nervous, Roz never having seen someone following death before looked shaky, we hugged trying not to cry. Leaning over to kiss Bren I saw Roz looking horrified 'why did you kiss her?' she said, I am acknowledging the love for my friend through the gesture and although this body housed her soul on earth she no longer needs it but spiritually she can see me. With that one of my phones rang, I was mortified and apologised having been certain that it was off. Looking at Bren serene in her coffin I said, 'sorry Bren I nearly had heart failure and joined you then'. Without warning the other phone turned on as though in response, we all laughed, I admonished

Bren affectionately knowing that she was playing with us. Saying our goodbyes to Bren was easier after that and as we entered the foyer I suggested to the girls that they walk up to the centre with me so we could have coffee together. I felt that they needed normal time to process and talk, they both agreed almost relieved.

There was a young woman walking down the stairs at the chapel, I looked at her and saw my friend's son standing beside her in spirit, the most handsome young man with big beautiful eyes and a cheeky face. He was pointing excitedly and saying, 'this is Julie (her name for now), she is brilliant and kind, she took care of me, she made my hair look good each time they got me out', he didn't seem the least bit perturbed or upset about being in spirit. Of course, I had to ask if she was Julie, she replied warily' yes I am' she was wide eyed when I said who had told me and that he was standing right beside her, I will call this beautiful young man Jacob for now. 'Jacob told me that you did 'last offices' for him when he arrived and he's very happy that you made sure his hair looked good each time he was brought out as he put it. You cried and talked to him with such kindness, I could see tears making their way to the brim of Julie's eyes as she remembered. Julies colleague came running from upstairs 'ooh! I love anything like this, sorry I couldn't help but hear'. As the two ladies stood together they were at first surrounded by babies that had briefly touched the earth, they had messages of gratitude for them. I told the ladies that the babies wished to thank them for lovingly caring for them and singing *wheels on the bus* to them. You held them and spoke to them as though they hadn't passed, you had soft brushes to do their hair and I smell talcum powder associated with newly bathed babies, they felt loved. Jacob asked me to tell the ladies that the girl who came in shortly after him was there as well, he described how she had passed, Jacob also told me how much comfort the ladies had given to bereaved families over the years and that they too were loved by those they had cared for.

I'm constantly in awe of people who tend the departed, cherishing them with dignity and respect from last offices to the chapel before finally ensuring that however rich or poor they were that they have a lovely service. After emotional goodbyes including to Jacob who stood watching as we left, we headed back to the centre. There on the pavement all the way to the centre were fluffy white angel feathers 'when a feather appears Angels are near' the pavement had been clear on my way to the chapel of rest. Not knowing the significance of white feather's, the girls asked why I was so excited by the angelic connection and gathered a pocket full of feathers each. While having coffee the girls talked about their homes in Poland, what had brought them to the UK and things they love, their work and hobbies. They needed to have normal chit chat to put things back in perspective and not be disturbed by the mornings events, it had been emotional. Before leaving I said 'Bren would have loved to be here enjoying girl talk and drinking coffee' with that one of my phones sprang into life again, the girls had watched me switch it off in the chapel. All three of us were in absolutely no doubt that Bren had joined us for coffee, it had been a morning of surprises. A time that should have been very sad but had brought validation of those we love being able to comfort us and make us smile from their new address. Thank you, Bren, and thank you Jacob, you really are special. Xxx

CHAPTER TWENTY-FOUR

It Really Is Ok To Cry

That night I met up with my friend, Jacobs Mum on night shift, she couldn't wait to tell me that she had spoken to Julie from the Funeral Company and was delighted. The two had become very close friends after bonding over Jacob's loss and the empathy Julie provided generously. Fliss, I will name her had deliberately not mentioned where Jacob had been taken to or given any details that I may have picked up on. Fully aware that we lived in different counties it was unlikely that I would be familiar with that chapel of rest or even know how many are dotted in and around that area.

I had seen Jacob standing next to Fliss several times when we first worked together but was wary of saying anything initially then when she told me that her son had passed tragically I was able to reassure her that he was around. Our friendship had been instant so it was joyful being able to pass on messages to Fliss even the random daft ones. Jacob asked me to tell Fliss off one day because he had watched as his Mum had moved heavy furniture from one part of a room to the other to decorate, he was fun, and we would both be cheered by his presence. Hopefully knowing how much Jacob is around all of her family Fliss will have some comfort because she is one of the nicest funniest hard working people I have in my life and her friendship is truly treasured. I have grown to love Jacob dearly so his photo goes with me overseas along with family photos inside my travel address book, his cheeky smile will never change. Fliss and I no longer work together but always felt that the events leading to our friendship were meant to be, I am forever grateful that this wonderful lady is in my life and love her dearly. Many people dream of winning the lottery, well one priority on my list would be to surprise Fliss with something that will enhance her life for the kindness she gives in abundance. Fliss grieves for her darling son every day, I see beyond the smile to the pain behind her eyes, yet she soldiers on not showing that pain to the world. Instead she gives support and laughter to every single person under the umbrella of her care, I could try for a hundred years to find fault with her and fail miserably.

Sadly though, it's that adage 'life goes on' and it does because it must, but one of the worst things in our culture is the lack of lasting compassion. It seems that once a funeral has taken place life should immediately get back to normal especially if that person isn't directly related. Yet we don't choose our family, but we do choose our friends, therefore the loss of a friend or close colleague for instance can be more painful than the loss of great uncle Egbert who has never been close and couldn't give a fig about anyone. Because grief isn't always acknowledged as a road of peaks and troughs that can take years to even out, the bereaved can get pushed to the kerb and forgotten. Grief can be all consuming often lasting for many years each one of us has a unique blend of coping strategies and emotional tolerance this needs to be recognised. I can give two examples off hand right now; Annie has been on several trips abroad and busied herself with running around for everyone and going to the theatre and cinema etc. as well as keeping her home going and dealing with unpleasant medical issues, since her dear husband passed a few years ago. Filling each day with escapism was her only way of coping with the immense loss of her practically childhood sweetheart. On the surface happy, bubbly full of energy and many other positives everyone assumed that she was doing well. But gradually she has become so worn out with pushing her grief away that it had started making her tired, then a tragic event happened to her best friend and that was the catalyst Knocking her for six? Annie is now completely exhausted and low, so she's able to allow the grief to manifest and give herself permission to heal when she is ready and however she chooses. We can basically say that her grief has only just begun but Annie had to handle her initial loss in the best way she could at the time in her own way, mostly because she didn't want to come across as needy or dependent, we know that she isn't either of those and just deserves our empathy and understanding because death of a loved one is the most difficult thing any of us has to face.

The second example is Jenny, she lost her husband around the same time as Annie, he is very prolific spiritually and leaves a lot of validation that he is around. Jenny is a successful business woman and had mostly a worry-free life with her doting husband who was everything to her. When he passed she was inconsolable, her grief was so deep that it practically stopped her ability to function. It seemed to her that her pain would never ease, and she struggled daily, her heartbreak evident in her face and demeanour. Then one event or incident after the other occurred without her 'man' beside her to make everything okay and through her pain she was forced to deal with a multitude of things that would test the strongest of characters. Jenny survived each majorly tough ordeal and I was privileged to see her grow in strength and begin to on good days look forward to the future. She still has a little way to go but she is blossoming and smiling in between the sad days. Both Ladies make me feel proud because I know in my heart of hearts that all will be good for both especially if they are surrounded by people who see beyond what shows on the surface. You can't go wrong with hugs, they speak volumes.

How much effort does it take to pop a little card or note in the post to let someone know that we are thinking of them with love? Something that they can pick up and read that tells them we sincerely care about how they are feeling. Social media has its place but how much more personal is even a simple home-made card or hand-written message especially if you know the bereaved well. However, saying that, many people acknowledge loss on social media to relative strangers because they have that lovely empathy anyway for those who are suffering. I am not knocking it because to acknowledge the loss of anyone whether in a personal way or via social media is still taking time out to show that you care. When we acknowledge the pain of someone's loss and recognise their grief it can be very healing for them. They may have lost the love of their life, a precious relative, dear friend, a child they could burst with love for, a wonderful colleague or neighbour. Although the levels of grief may differ the pain is real.

'They're in a far better place now', although meant well doesn't always help, someone suffering bereavement does not want their loved one to be in a far better place regardless of suffering. Irrationally, given the pain a loved one is released from following death, many would still give anything for them to stay.

Whereas for example 'I am so sad that this has happened and can barely imagine how you are feeling or how painful it is for you', is perhaps more apt. If you can't manage the words to express your sadness to someone remember a hug says a thousand words, tears are nothing to be ashamed of, love and empathy matter.

Because you are reading this there is a good chance that you trust in spirit or are at the very least curious and probably agree that there is certainly something very special. You may not be able to grasp what it is now but how wonderful that our loved ones are with us sending signs for us to acknowledge their presence.

CHAPTER TWENTY-FIVE

Accepting Heavenly Signs

Signs present in many forms and someone once asked 'why robins'? so I said 'look at how cute robins are for a start, with their little hi there! attitude and confidence tamely watching or walking up close to us.

Compare a dear cute robin to a big fat pigeon depositing its vast amount of bowel contents all over the place while flapping noisy wings.

If I were in higher life eager to visit my 'rellies' on earth I most certainly wouldn't choose for part of my soul to visit them via a pooping pigeon that would just make them cross. Robins have been loved and recognised spiritually for a very long time as have butterflies, dragonflies and rainbows etc. nature is healing and perfect for connecting with spirit. Once you are aware and accepting of signs it can be very comforting, I'm not an expert by any means but I trust in the daily signs sent to me and can only pass them on.

Cherishing our angels and not underestimating how much they love and want to help us is very enlightening, I can give you an example of how they made one of my therapy clients feel in her hour of need.

Several years ago, now it was a Wednesday morning about 11-00 a m, I had been grocery shopping after night shift and was putting the last few bits away when there was a halfhearted knock at the door. There in a crumpled heap on the step was a young woman sobbing her heart out, she couldn't speak as her chest heaved with the force of her sobs. Helping her to her feet my first instinct was to hug her close to me then I led her into the house and made a cup of tea. Over tea I understood that she was suffering from severe depression so once I had ascertained that she would be free for a few hours a plan of action emerged.

Soon we were in my car heading for Hatfield Forest with a picnic and having parked near to the picnic area and small shop we walked to the lake sat down on a cosy blanket and ate together it was good to see her eat because she probably hadn't had anything substantial for a good few hours making her sugar levels low and subsequently her mood. Neither of us spoke for a while, we absorbed the surroundings and the warmth, the animal and bird sounds, rippling lake water and children giggling, we watched butterflies and a weird variety of flying insects performing acrobats as if for our benefit. Our food seemed to taste better outdoors, my companion appeared relaxed nature was waving her healing wand eager to help this poor young woman with whatever lay so heavy in her head. The picnic bag and blanket were put back in the car and once more we walked to the lake then alongside it onto the wooden decked pathway meandering through the forest. As we walked she poured her broken heart to me, crying in between sentences and expressing small bursts of angry frustration. We sat down on a fallen tree trunk for a while and I sensed her sheer exhaustion from the effort of having offloaded so much pent-up emotion. Hugging her I thanked her for trusting and sharing, she told me that she felt drawn towards my house as though invisible hands were pulling her. 'There are three ways to get back to the car that I know of', I pointed them out 'which one would you choose?' A lovely smile appeared 'the middle one'. The path she chose was initially through bushes before the area opened to reveal lumpy bits of field leading to the narrow roadway we had driven on earlier. As we set off tripping over clumps of earth and weeds we both spotted the smallest fluffiest white feathers at our feet and gathered them up. The feathers were lain front of us, however much the rugged field caused us to sidestep, all the way along our route they were dotted in front of us and we laughed. Approaching my car, the pathway of feathers had stopped abruptly at the passenger door, we looked at each other as the realisation hit us, and we just knew that she was going to be alright. That dear young woman going home was a completely different one to the one crumpled up on my doorstep, such is the power of angels and nature. No longer a troubled soul she's able to recognise triggers to her depression clearly and we have worked together to form positive coping strategies. My picnic companion trusts in spirit and her angels without any prompting and I'm proud of her for embracing everything good in her life as she realises what a fabulous and strong woman she is.

CHAPTER TWENTY-SIX

Simply 'Bob' A Good Man

Several days on from Hatfield Forest it was the funeral of a very special much-loved man, the husband of another amazing lady I am proud to have as a friend. Arriving on a vintage fire vehicle the coffin was proudly delivered to the funeral location for a service that had packed the chapel to capacity as family, friends and colleagues poured inside. Many more straining to hear the eulogy and lovely tributes from outside mourning yet celebrating the life of a good man, loved by so many. Standing in the foyer with old friends and colleagues around me I silently asked my angels to please help the family through such an emotional day. Within seconds, I heard the voice of my friend's husband it seemed loud to me but looking at people near to me it was obvious that it was for my ears only. 'They've given me a bloody good send-off it's great', he asked me to let his 'girls' meaning my friend and their daughters, know that he treasured what was placed in the coffin and it made him laugh when they put his hat on. Not a habitual hat wearer, the hat was worn when working on cars in the yard, a great passion of his. He had laughed about the hat and loved the service they ran over to their mum excitedly relating the message, because it was all as their Dad had said and they knew I had never seen him in a hat. A very simple random message but worth such a lot to the 'girls' because they loved him.

CHAPTER TWENTY-SEVEN

Pony Tail Man

'Do you and Paul fancy lunch with us on Saturday?' said our friend's lovely voice down the phone, 'wonderful' was my excited reply. Life was busy with barely enough time to breathe so the luxury of having a social meal was something to look forward to.

M and R ran a very popular old-fashioned Inn with loads of character, not knowing the history surrounding such a fantastic place we were looking forward to enjoying the ambience as much as the company and food. No sooner had we been seated than I saw a man wandering around and immediately realised that he was not of this earth but was a spiritual being. Hands on hips he had a bemused air of arrogance, his straggly hair was tied back in a ponytail and his teeth were bad, there was a pouch purse dangling from his belt and he wore a tricorn hat. He knew that I could see him, looking around it was apparent no one else could see him including Paul. M came over to sit with us and smiled sheepishly when I asked her about the man. We chatted about family then I visualized 'pony tail' man helping another man to lift a motionless figure up inside the huge open fireplace, hoist him onto a hook then laugh. No one paid any attention to their weird behavior my suspicion that 'pony tail' man and partner in crime were visitors of a supernatural kind was confirmed, I did my best to ignore them.

We were drinking coffee after lunch when the same man appeared in a booth at the far side of the Inn slamming chunky discs of metal onto the table from his pouch purse. Spotting my puzzled face, he would have gained pleasure at the discomfort he was causing, of course he was fully aware that I knew his happy face was just a façade he was in fact a very bad man.

M asked us to walk through the bar areas with her and in the area near to the booth a distinct sound of pigs squealing came to me, I sensed a gutter full of blood and a trapdoor nearby. 'Pony tail' man told me that a letter had been written about him that not many people had seen, he was quite jovial and friendly, but I wasn't in a hurry to trust him or become 'besties'. Absolutely delighted, M said she'd hoped I would pick up on 'pony tail' man then admit to us that one of the reasons she wanted us to have lunch there was in the hope that I would pick up on none other than Dick Turpin. To say that I was shocked is an understatement, but what the heck in for a penny in for a pound. Paul was beside himself and kept joking 'my pal Dick Turpin, cheers mate what are you up to these days?' I will be honest I can't tell you for sure that it was Dick Turpin my ego isn't big enough to accept for certain that it was him even with everything pointing towards it being him. Knowing how powerful some spiritual energy is and not wishing to encourage or absorb anything bad or negative I asked Paul not to joke, a cheeky grin back told me he wasn't finished making me squirm.

We were shown the chimney space behind the fireplace where the hook was and told that near the booth was a trapdoor to the cellar at one time. It is suspected that Dick Turpin prolific Highway robber used to dispose of bodies via the trapdoor where they would be wheeled away by barrow to an abattoir close by and dealt with. The letter was shown to us and true to Dick's word had not been shown to many people. It had been framed and kept safe following authentication as an historic artefact. R (who did all the cooking for our yummy meal) and M (who that day just looked beautiful) thanked us warmly for having lunch there and checking out areas of the Inn where staff had experienced strange things like glasses flying off the bar and things being moved. We in turn thanked them for a delicious late lunch/ early dinner and for a very different form of entertainment not to mention an on the spot history lesson. It was early evening as we were leaving, a strange phenomenon began to occur, the sky went pitch black not a star twinkling or glimpse of moonlight, eerie. Paul piped up with 'where's my pal Dick Turpin when we need him? Turning the car around to face the right direction was no mean feat without a particle of light to guide us, the headlights seemed weaker too. Seconds later the road ahead was lit up, we gasped 'thanks mate' Paul called out presumably to his new pal the notorious highway robber. 'Paul it isn't often that I get cross but please don't encourage bad spirits we can't have him in our house', my pleas fell on deaf ears and only spurred him on.

Strangely though by some coincidence (or was it?) all of our route home, quite a distance from the Inn was brightly lit up, parking in our drive I said' thank you for your help in guiding us home safely but now I would like you to return to where you came from'. Before Paul could say a thing, I stopped him in his tracks, the light uncannily disappeared, and the sky was black once again, as we went indoors we had to ask each other if it really was D T helping or just a weird occurrence. Personally, I like to think that our guardian angels were protecting us.

I could only ask our angels to keep us safe, I thanked them.

CHAPTER TWENTY-EIGHT

Miranda

My next story shows how diverse spirituality can be and accepting it only for the higher good can build a protective instinct.

Many years ago, I was asked to cover an Agency night shift some distance from my home, details were limited but as a Sagittarian with Nomadic traits I had no sense of trepidation or concern. To me it was never just work but a new adventure too.

The house was magnificent standing proudly in lovely grounds it was a good feeling realising that my patient had such beautiful surroundings as aid to her recovery. In answer to the tuneful doorbell came a lady who swung open the Gothic style door with a welcoming smile. Introducing myself and presenting ID as usual the lady nodded approvingly then said that not only was she the patient's neighbour but a friend of many years. Entering the house I was shown into a room immediately on the left of the spacious hallway, it was a cosy sitting room tastefully furnished with additional homely items like television, a full bookcase and big squidgy cushions. Leading off from the sitting room was a gorgeous bedroom with en suite bathroom, another door led to a compact but fully functioning kitchen and larder stocked with enough food to feed a football team. The lady then said that while I was nursing her friend this would be my apartment and it would be wonderful if I could feel at home, feel at home! I had my bags packed mentally to move in. She then led me through to an incredibly designed lounge where we were seated while discussing the nursing plan and care notes, I was then told a little of the background prior to the patient's illness. I have decided to call her Miranda rather than to keep referring to her as 'my or the patient' she deserves an identity.

Miranda it seems had been a very prominent figure in the City, holding a highly esteemed position when an incident had occurred putting her life in the gravest of danger. Without being too detailed and sparing the graphics it impacted on Miranda's life hugely. Shortly afterwards Miranda began losing her short term memory whereas she had always been as sharp as a tack prior to the incident. Invariably Miranda had no choice but to resign from her high-profile job much to her dismay.

Neighbour's being so spread about were unaware that Miranda was at home alone apart from her three cats and they were accustomed to her absence therefore no one was concerned; her friend had been away caring for her mother.

Meanwhile Miranda was presenting with signs of Post Traumatic Syndrome Distress plus the onset of Dementia, both such cruel conditions not always understood.

Miranda's friend returned home after a lengthy absence and immediately popped around to see her, she had peered through one of the expansive floors to ceiling stained glass windows and recoiled in shock at the sight before her. Miranda was dangerously emaciated and practically at deaths door, an ambulance was called, and she was in hospital for over a month without any living relatives to visit with words of comfort.

You know that feeling you have when someone is not being completely honest? Well, that was the feeling I had, probably nothing to do with psychic ability more likely body language and lack of eye contact as the conversation carried on. As long as there was enough information and the medical notes were clear I could cope with that unless it had potential to prevent quality patient care. We continued the house tour. Wow! The kitchen was to die for and on close inspection had been cleverly designed for practicality and ease of access. Fascinating cookery books from all over the world plus an abundance of professional level gadgets and exotic spices gave an inkling that Miranda either loved cooking passionately or she had a very adventurous housekeeper. Miranda's house was a building so perfectly designed with taste and love that each room was a joy to behold.

What was totally alien to me is that my psychic 'oooerrr! something isn't right radar' had vamoosed. Memo to self, Valerie wake up and taste the coffee or smell the roses whatever, you are not super woman with amazing senses so get over yourself and snatch back that ego. Of course, *I Am Me, No One Special* I must remember that because to treasure the little gift of second sight I inherited from Grandma Willis, ego is harmful and has no place in the world of spirit. I was proud and so sure of my ability to pick up negative energy in absolutely any building that contained it, practically the minute I entered. Yet there I was at Miranda's and my feelings had registered zilch. Something that was to change dramatically a few hours later, when my 'mojo' returned with a vengeance. It was fascinating walking around and I felt privileged to be spoken to like a friend by the neighbour who showed off the lovely home as proudly as though it was her own. Upstairs were four bedrooms each with en suite facilities including Miranda's, there was a small study room across the landing facing Miranda's bedroom. Miranda's case study notes and care plan were on the desk for staff to log after each relevant action along with meds and so on. All ready for staff handover. It was that room I decided to spend the night in rather than the pretty apartment, to me night shifts are a good opportunity to bond with patient's. They are more likely to open about how they feel when one to one, interruption free. They can have 100% nurturing they also have the security of having someone alert ready to spring into action in an emergency.

Next came the introduction to Miranda who also opened her greeting with a welcome smile, she shook my hand eagerly, hazel eyes scrutinised, not unpleasantly just curious. Miranda's hair was steel grey and immaculately coiffed, her lips thin with a smear of tinted lip balm she was in her seventies, with a timeless classical air about her. In front of me was a lady who would never lose the impressive look of someone highly regarded, however cruel Dementia chipped away at her. The underlying aura of authority was deeply imprinted, Miranda carried it with pride.

The friend reminded me that I was free to go anywhere in the house then before leaving handed a list of Miranda's likes and dislikes. At the door she hugged me tightly thanking me profusely saying she knew that I was the right person to be with Miranda.

Notes and care plans all read, meds sorted, hot chocolate for Miranda who was in her night wear, pillows all fluffed and comfy, perfect, all in time for an intro chat. A very intelligent lady who spoke of her reluctant retirement from the super powered career she had thrived on. All so normal, a fascinating lady indeed and appreciative that she would have someone at close quarters throughout the night, admitted that she often suffered from night terrors.

While Miranda was reading for a while I decided to see if there were any little jobs I could do to make life easier for the day staff. They had left a half-finished pile of ironing neatly folded on a chair in the lounge so once Miranda was settled for the night I got stuck into it, listening as I did so to the intercom connection from upstairs.

I had begun to feel very uneasy and nauseous the warm room felt decidedly cooler and strange noises were coming through the intercom. Worst of all was the vile smell of rotting flesh or dead animals that had started to permeate the room, growing stronger. I had goosebumps on my arms and couldn't understand what was happening when everything had seemed so perfect.

Walking briskly towards the wide wooden staircase I could hear cats plaintively mewing, it was heartbreaking. Little shapes appeared all over the stairs, cats! Cats! That's what they were cats! Oh my goodness some were whole, some emaciated carcasses. Blood and dried blood appeared, faeces and urine it was too awful, was spirit trying to expand on the story partly told?

Running upstairs to check on Miranda she was no longer lucid and was mumbling incoherently, her notes had stated that Dementia saw her lapsing at intervals before returning to lucidity and able to communicate therefore I wasn't too concerned. Prescription anti-anxiety meds were taken, and she soon settled seemingly none the worse for her episode and unaware of mine.

Downstairs it was as though nothing had happened, ironing finished coffee in hand I went to the study room opposite Miranda's bedroom. It was 01-45 Miranda had been checked, she was sleeping soundly the meds having kicked in nicely. Night log updated omitting certain events, who would believe it anyway? time to get stuck into studying. The nature of my work stipulates continued education and updates to keep the professional level I need to continue at, complacency is never an option.

It must have been around 03-00 a m when some type of presence seemed to be there as I sat hunched over my study books in the room opposite Miranda's, the soft glow from a table lamp in the room was the only light. First the slight chill like a psychic breeze followed by a veritable rush of movement from behind me coming from the window wall area and passing towards the open door. My studying was too necessary to look around at a mischievous spirit so the black shadows that had whizzed past in a flash were only glimpsed out of the corner of my eye. Thankfully the last few hours were incident free, one refreshed, fed, medicated patient later I prepared for handover, my duty of care at an end.

Greeting me in the kitchen was the friend who was there to fill the gap between agency staff. It was obvious from her body language that that she was curious to see if something had happened in fact she looked relieved that I was relaxed and cheerful. Sipping her coffee Miranda's friend looked as though she was bursting to say something, so I just took the bull by the horns and asked outright what had happened in the house.

Evidently when Miranda had been forced into retirement following the huge incident she had become reclusive. Suffering from anxiety attacks and PTSD, her behaviour had rocketed, she would walk for miles each night in the dark collecting cats in a wheelie shopping bag. The cats had the run of the house and were fed until the food ran out, the once splendidly beautiful house was rank with the smell of rotting cat flesh and blood where they had attacked each other, faeces and urine soaked the carpets with ammonia.

When Miranda was discovered the scene was reminiscent of a murder scene. Miranda was covered in blood, vomit and faeces, the bites and scratches she had received were infected, she was days from death. After a lengthy stay in hospital with psychiatric assessments and good counselling she was allowed home and the nightmares became less. Dementia had become her friend in many ways because it had chased away the terrible darkness that had made her ill. Love and life in her later years were healing giving peace in her once again splendid home.

I prayed that the residual energy I had experienced did not affect Miranda too, her friend and I hugged goodbye, an understanding had been formed one hard to explain to anyone. I believe the cats had sought me out as an empath to validate them in spirit, which is why I couldn't sense negative energy. They will be at peace now and will definitely have been given healing as they passed. Love and light to their dear little souls. Once home I phoned Lynette to ask her about the dark shadows that had rushed behind me in the study room, 'bless you darling' she said, I am just glad that you didn't turn around to look at the shadow people, they were there because the tragedy left behind deep residual energy', adding ' so sad darling about the lady and her cats how very tragic '. I hadn't told her anything at all about Miranda or the cats but as a powerful trance medium she just knew, such is our bond.

CHAPTER TWENTY-NINE

Daniel Robinson

This is an event that changed our life forever, God Bless Daniel Robinson, sometimes misunderstood but always loving and forever loved, our little entrepreneur building his empire fit for a King in Heaven.

On the 1st of May 2017 the emergency phone in our bedroom rang, it was loud and startling, the clock ticking away showed the time as 04-00 a m, at that time it could only be bad news. 'Valerie its Caroline, Daniel's been found dead', it was Daniel's Mum her chilling message delivered calmly with no words wasted, she was numb with shock. Suddenly, wide awake I jumped up' Oh my God no please no, have you got anyone with you? I'm worried about you, where are you now? It was all such a painful blur. Paul woke up and I wished with all of my heart that what he was about to be told was just a bad dream that we would awaken from. 'What's happened, is it Mum or Dad?' how do you tell a father that his son had been found dead in tragic circumstances, knowing that his heart would be broken? Caroline had spent hours with

Daniel before she had the strength to call us, she was distraught, there were no words to comfort her and make it right for her, he would always be her baby boy, she was lost. Paul was absolutely broken in pieces, still his little soldier even though he was a young adult with his own business, he loved his son heart and soul. We got up, shock waves washing over us as we struggled to register such devastating news, too shocked even to cry we held each other in disbelief. 'We can't phone your Mum and Dad at this time in the morning sweetheart, they are too poorly' I almost whispered, Paul was certain that his brother Mark would answer the phone so before dawn had broken that day they were told that their cheeky grandson had died.

My three children were told at breakfast time and as a family we mourned the loss of Paul and Caroline's elder son, my handsome stepson and adored brother to my children, it was beyond painful.

Daniel's younger brother Nic stepped up to be strong for his mum despite his own crippling grief. Anyone dealing with bereavement knows that there is such a lot to do at a time when emotions steal all but the last shred of energy and zap the thought processes. Caroline kept us updated every step of the way, we all struggled and were in limbo until the funeral, each of us going through the motions. Caroline wanted to choose Daniels service and place of rest, we fully understood, it was her last act as Daniel's Mum and vitally important, her heart and soul went into the arrangements and it showed.

The weekend before the funeral was beautiful, it was sunny, and flowers bloomed everywhere, Paul wanted to do a reccy to the church and crematorium to work out travel times etc., so that's what we did.

Parking outside the church we tried not to cry as we decided where we would park on the day. Our next stop was back through the town up to the crematorium and because it was Sunday lunchtime the car park nearest the chapel was empty. As we stepped from the car the most overwhelming feeling of peace enveloped me letting me know that the grounds were full of love. I heard children singing loudly as they played 'Ring a Ring of Roses', they laughed and it filled my heart with joy. 'Sweetheart isn't it lovely hearing the children playing over there?' 'where? I can't hear anything' was his puzzled response, Sometimes Paul has difficulty hearing, so I just smiled. Walking around, Daniel's presence was reassuring me to be strong for his Dad, we had to exit a different way and I pointed excitedly to an area in front of us, 'that's where the children were singing see if they are still there'. As we approached the area the little road veered so that the place I had pointed to was on our left. The whole of that area was a cemetery dedicated to babies and children who'd passed, it surely was a haven of great love where spirit children come out to play.

It seems strangely weird to state that I love the grounds there but it's true, we vowed that as soon as we were strong enough to walk the grounds we would go back. We dressed in silence on the day of the funeral afraid to speak in case the floodgate of tears threatened to spill, words were not important we hugged instead, we knew how we felt and the pain every one of us was sharing, our thoughts and prayers were with Nic as well as Caroline. Daniel was my stepson and I loved him as though he was a child of my own, but never once underestimated how much harder it was for Paul and Caroline. Thankful that Caroline had family support we set off with trepidation towards the church. Approaching a small roundabout in town barely noticing our surroundings Paul cried out, he had spotted a stunning white wood and glass carriage with two magnificent horses. The pale blue coffin with painted doves on it was being gently placed into the carriage with the 'Me to You' teddy bear wreath Paul had chosen with so much love. Both of us burst into tears' it's our Daniel babe, it's our boy' we sobbed without control and missed the turn off to the church, it was such a shock to come across him then and so unprepared. Daniel arrived at the church and the service was perfect, Father knew Daniel well, so the service was conducted with love and affection. Through the town Daniel led the procession, people bowed their heads, blew kisses, saluted and even stood quietly in respect, their compassion warmed us we were really touched.

Father also did the committal service then when it was over everybody mingled in the glorious sunshine to look at the wonderful tributes, the compassionate Funeral Director who knew Daniel very well made everything beautiful and personal. I learned that day that he too had heard the spirit children playing. We are truly privileged and feel certain that Daniel totally approves of his Mum's perfect choices, we certainly do. Paul and I are extremely proud of Caroline for creating an outstanding day of love, it really was incredibly beautiful.

The evening after Daniel's funeral Paul was standing by our lounge door and Daniel's outline appeared to Paul's right-hand side, vanishing literally in seconds, it made me gasp in surprise, but Paul cannot cuddle an apparition so knowing would not have given any comfort at all just then. In the weeks following, several small things happened quite randomly, some of which I did mention to Paul, others I gratefully accepted as loving signs from Daniel. During one very down time for Paul I did Angel cards and asked if I could have a special message from Daniel just for his Dad. Paul returned from work he'd been crying as he was driving, he hugged me and emotionally stated 'I keep thinking that it's all my fault' I handed the angel card to him that was in my hand, it clearly read 'It's not your fault'. Bearing in mind that card came from a pack which is one of around 28 packs all different, what are the odds of that card appearing?' Paul has never doubted that the message of reassurance was from his son.

Daniel loved Me to You, Tatty Teddy Bears so for his birthday I made a special card and framed it for him to see on his earthly visits. One day Paul was coping well but my emotions were all over the place so rather than open his wounds I went upstairs and because I was thinking of Daniel the feeling of loss for his physical presence was overwhelming. Talking aloud I said

'Daniel, I know that I'm not your real Mum darling, but I love you like my own sons and miss you so much. Pulling myself together I popped into my craft room to put some die cut shapes away, a minute later I went to brush something from my left elbow and was stunned to see that it was a cute Me to You 3D embellishment stuck firmly to me. I hadn't any left where did it come from?'. Smiling to myself I carried on then felt something uncomfortable jam in between my left little toe and the one next to it, extracting the crumpled piece of card, it was astounding with just one word on it in bold letters 'MUM'. Running downstairs to tell Paul trying to process what happened at the same time it was so good. Caroline will always be Daniel's Mum, she was generous and allowed me to share him, so for him to acknowledge my love means that he was aware of it. We have chosen to accept and embrace these wonderful signs.

I don't worry about Daniel now because he is loved, and his memorial plaque is in almost his own little kingdom. Whenever we go there we leave angel feathers and that huge feeling of peace gently surrounds us. Paul finds some comfort in knowing that his son is reaching out to him and chats away happily to him, however if Daniel suddenly appeared in front of Paul he would most likely stop breathing. The mischievous side of Daniel will be chuckling at that thought but the caring side loved his Dad so much that scaring him is not an option. I think that anyone who has been bereaved has days when the physical loss is unbearable, being unable to hug their loved one or hear their voice can be debilitating, it then becomes difficult to accept that our loved ones are close, but they are, just look for signs and listen.

Our Daniel was called far too soon, snatched without warning and there is a huge Daniel sized void, but we have a lot of loving signs for which we are truly thankful, and we continue to be as positive as possible to give strength to others.

CHAPTER THIRTY

SPOOKY?

Sitting beside Paul on the sofa writing out an
endless 'to do' list I worried about him being home
alone with only Cherry 'Diva 'dog for company and
time to dwell during my due trip to Mumbai that
October. Anyway, at Paul's insistence I put those
thoughts to one side and suddenly remembered
that I needed to message Father Noel in Mumbai,
something totally unrelated to Daniel. Tapping away
on my phone in lower casing suddenly in front of me
on the screen was the name Daniel in upper casing,
because it was surprising I just deleted it then told
Paul but was really frustrated at not having shown
it to him first. Paul trusted me, I started again, and
there once more was DANIEL, shaking I showed it
to Paul insisting that it was probably predictive text
or something, swearing that it wasn't deliberate. 'I
know that you would never do something like that
sweetheart and besides I watched you type your
message, how does Dear Father Noel suddenly
translate to just one-word DANIEL?' we may not
know but it was a wow! moment even if it was
predictive text. Those of you who are technically

minded are probably smiling now and thinking Bless em! they haven't got a clue, it was just nice.

It made a refreshing change for me because my predictive texts often come up as hilariously rude even though my messages vary between normal and boring.

CHAPTER THIRTY-ONE

Magnificent
Iridescent Wings

Dear Barbara, precious truly loved friend and one-time beloved Mother Superior mentioned earlier well bless her heart she had deteriorated health wise throughout 2016 and 2017culminating in her sad passing in November 2017. Barbara's funeral was held in December at St. Elizabeth's her Holy home in Much Hadham, it was attended by family and close friends. Most of the service washed over me because it was difficult to see and hear the Priest clearly instead I gave in to affectionate thoughts of the funny lady we would never see again in this life time. Barbara's beautiful Daughter in law stood at the front to talk about her and the two men blocking my view moved position enough for me to see her as she spoke. Carol was eloquent and beautiful, her words loving and sincere, listening intently my eyes were drawn to her when suddenly something happened that never in my wildest of dreams could I have predicted. It was a moment so unbelievably amazing that it took my breath away and to describe accurately what occurred is difficult.

Throughout my life I have believed in Angels and trusted in the love they surround us with, translating Angel cards is as natural to me as breathing, my love of Angels is well known. Yet I had never knowingly seen an Angel face to face as it were or in the many ways that people in spirit appear to me, it never diminishes belief or trust as there is so much more that has promoted acceptance.

As Carol continued speaking, a shape was forming behind her, my feelings were that it was female, there was a very delicate sense to the vision appearing before my eyes. Magnificent iridescent wings formed in hues of lilac, silver and turquoise, a face so undeniably beautiful emerged from the layers that had formed wings. Was I awake had I passed to spirit surely everyone could see her, it was impossible not to see this lady resplendent in spiritual colours, lighting the whole area like a magical illusion.

What was wrong with everyone? How could they not be moved by such a mind-blowing experience, then it struck me they just couldn't see her. Why me? worst case scenario I was going crackers, I mean 7 feet tall and glowing isn't exactly something to be ignored. As fast as doubt crept in I threw it away, then looking across at two of St Elizabeth's elderly residents away from the main congregation in wheelchairs it was clear that one was mesmerised and pointing right in the direction of the Angel. Holding out her arms quietly her face told me that what she was seeing was shared with two of us that day. Still in the pinch me quick zone I listened to Joan's grandson talking about Barbara (aunty Barbara) he had my full attention. Having spoken to his Mum Carolyn earlier I knew that he was really nervous but he seemed very confident. Then I saw why, Barbara stood in between him and the Priest, resolutely blowing kisses to everyone with the biggest smile on her face. At the graveside the immense grief I'd expected to be overwhelming didn't appear, instead it was a feeling of euphoria. Dear Barbara, had been called home. During the wake Carolyn's son shared with me that he had sensed Barbara's presence in church and he was sure that I had seen her too. Reading the faces of my friends it was clear that each one trusted me, and I learned why. Describing the spectacular vision, I'd seen they all smiled and said they were happy because the Angels would have come for her. Evidently all of Barbara's life she has believed in Angels and they visited her many times as a child and an adult, she always said that she was blessed, now I know why. With such amazing experiences and moments, I am forever grateful for the fabulous events that Spirit, and my Angels have allowed me to be privy to. They have moulded my character, giving me huge inner strength to help people, something I am passionate about. Daniel continues to leave signs and we never doubt any of them so I hope and pray that you too are able to recognise and accept the signs your loved ones send to you, with the understanding that they haven't left you, they have just changed address Wishing you love and inner peace.

I Continue to Be Me, No One Special.

In love and light, In love and light, In love and light.

Note from the Author

I chose to write this book because so many of you have struggled through your own experiences, hopefully by reading about mine you can relate to yours positively and stay strong just as I have. Maybe because *I Am Me, No One Special* I did let that nasty 'P' word creep in, after all why would anyone want to read about my life I'm ordinary and I shop at Tesco's? But don't you find that we often under estimate people and the impact they can have on us such is the tapestry of life?

It was a weekday morning and a friend Geraldine Morris popped in to chat; we invariably got on to the subject of all things spiritual. To describe Gerry my first word would be colourful, her clothes, hair and personality are fabulously unique to Gerry and her spiritual energy positively basks in the glory of her personality. Gerry didn't encourage me to finish the notes I had made for a potential book on spiritual events, she told me outright that I had to crack on with it because she wanted to read it. 'No excuses just do it' she said and trust me she meant it. Her aura glowed, her eyes bright and determined Gerry believed that I could write such a book after all auras don't lie. Well, within minutes of her leaving pen and paper poised I started writing again as though my life depended on it and the memories poured into my head. Geraldine Morris, you were the rainbow catalyst that helped to change my 'P' word from procrastination to positive giving me the push I needed and my gratitude knows no bounds, I love you for it, thank you xxxxxxx

My dear partner Paul Robinson (Furbyroops), your love and support never wavered for a second, your kindness and encouragement were constant, your generosity amazing. Grateful thanks too for the chocolate administered at regular intervals (medicinal of course), I am so lucky.

Sylvia and Ken (Mum and Dad Robinson), for loving me as the daughter you never had and being beyond patient through my endless work and study commitments. Mark Robinson, my brother from another mother, fantastic portrait artist, you let me run my crazy ideas past you and illustrated one of my hand made project books for India.

Annie Sutton, Zoe Tivey and Jenny Myhill for reading some of my notes with great patience.

Russell and Jean Cottis for being there at the right time showing wonderful support, I will never forget your kindness.

Love to Bruce and Wendy Haynes plus everyone else walking in my footsteps, you know who you are but it doesn't hurt to know that you are appreciated.

Terence Watts (Mega Qualifications), my amazing tutor, mentor and inspiration for over sixteen years, to be taught by you is a huge privilege, your knowledge is vast and studying with you is fun. This book won't surprise you Terence because you know me so well. Thank you Terence for all you have enabled me to be.

My heart is filled with gratitude for the spiritual guidance that led me to Spiderwize. Right from my very first conversations with Haylee Brown and Leanne Hyland their support has been constantly invaluable. From day one I was advised and encouraged 100% always with kindness and friendship. The initial evaluation of my manuscript by Jenny Do Carmo was really positive and gave me a huge confidence boost. The whole process has been exciting and I appreciate every single one of the fabulous Spiderwize family whatever their role in making this humble book a reality, thank you.

With much love, Valerie xxxxxx

Lightning Source UK Ltd.
Milton Keynes UK
UKHW050157190322
400211UK00015B/772